BACKTOTHEBIBLE.CA

HEAVEN

AND

HELL

DR. JOHN NEUFELD

Heaven and Hell
Copyright © 2024 by The Good News
Broadcasting Association of Canada

All rights reserved. No part of this publication may be reproduced, distributed, or transmitted in any form or by any means, including photocopying, recording, or other electronic or mechanical methods, without the prior written permission of the author, except in the case of brief quotations embodied in critical reviews and certain other non-commercial uses permitted by copyright law. For permission requests, permissions@gnbac.ca

Scripture quotations are from the ESV® Bible (The Holy Bible, English Standard Version®), © 2001 by Crossway, a publishing ministry of Good News Publishers. Used by permission. All rights reserved. The ESV text may not be quoted in any publication made available to the public by a Creative Commons license. The ESV may not be translated in whole or in part into any other language.

ISBN
978-1-7388135-7-5 (Hardcover)
978-1-7388135-6-8 (Paperback)
978-1-7388135-8-2 (eBook)

Quotations used with permission:

Jonathan Edwards, The Works, Volume 1.
Edinburgh: The Banner of Truth Trust, 1974. Page 20.

Jonathan Edwards, The Works, Volume 2.
Edinburgh: The Banner of Truth Trust, 1974. Page 902.

Reflections on the Psalms by C.S. Lewis
© copyright 1958 C.S. Lewis Pte Ltd

The Weight of Glory by C.S. Lewis © copyright 1949 C.S. Lewis Pte Ltd

The Problem of Pain by C.S. Lewis © copyright 1940 C.S. Lewis Pte Ltd

Letters to Malcolm: Chiefly on Prayer by C.S. Lewis
© copyright 1963, C.S. Lewis Pte Ltd.
Extracts used with permission.

Some content taken from Heaven by Randy Alcorn. Copyright © 2004. Used by permission of Tyndale House Publishers. All rights reserved.

Taken from Systematic Theology by Wayne Grudem. Copyright © 1994 by Wayne Grudem. Used by permission of HarperCollins Christian Publishing. www.harpercollinschristian.com.

TABLE OF CONTENTS

FOREWORD 1
INTRODUCTION 3
Chapter 1   THE REALITY OF DEATH 9
Chapter 2   COMING TO TERMS WITH HEAVEN AND HELL 20
Chapter 3   THINKING THE UNTHINKABLE 30
Chapter 4   HELL AND THE NATURE OF GOD 41
Chapter 5   THE AWFUL NATURE OF HELL 53
Chapter 6   A FEW REMAINING QUESTIONS 64
Chapter 7   WHAT HAPPENS WHEN A BELIEVER DIES? 74
Chapter 8   THE INTERMEDIATE STATE 86
Chapter 9   THE FINAL JUDGMENT 98
Chapter 10 A NEW HEAVEN AND A NEW EARTH 109
Chapter 11 THE RESURRECTION OF THE BODY 119
Chapter 12 SEEING GOD FACE TO FACE 130
Chapter 13 RULING AND REIGNING WITH CHRIST 139
Chapter 14 GOING ON FOR ETERNITY 150
Chapter 15 CONCLUSION 161

FOREWORD

As a boy growing up in a Christian home and church, I recall often hearing about the realities of Heaven and Hell. "Prophecy conferences" were popular in those days, and they often included treatments about the joys of Heaven and the horrors of Hell. Of course, not all of these messages were appropriately delivered, nor were all as faithful to the Scriptures as they should have been. But much about them got things right—there is a real Heaven of joy and fulfillment for those who trust in Christ alone for the forgiveness of their sins, and who know He is the only hope for eternal life. There is also a real Hell for all others outside of Christ, in which separation from God will mean everlasting misery.

For whatever reason, the prevalent awareness of the Heaven and Hell of those days has passed. As John Neufeld aptly points out, our antiseptic age often softens the reality of death while offering little if any consideration about what lies beyond. If anything, a general assumption can be detected from time to time that all go to Heaven, so there are no worries about Hell, at least for most people. If there is a Hell at all, it is sparsely populated with only the worst of the worst. Hitler might be there, but normal folk can count on Heaven, if such things actually exist.

Readers of this excellent treatment of Heaven and Hell will find out how sorely mistaken so many in our culture are about these realities. And it's not just people in our culture generally who are clueless to the truths about what lies beyond the grave, many in the church have been injected with the same inoculation that prevents them from seriously considering subjects like divine wrath and judgment. As a result, they simply do not know how crucially important these areas of study are for their own lives and those of whom they love. In short, we today really, genuinely, deeply need a corrective to the lazy and sloppy neglect and ignorance of one of the most important questions: what happens when this life is over?

I am grateful to John Neufeld, seasoned pastor and Bible teacher, for taking the time and effort to write the insightful and instructive chapters of this book. His clarity and biblical fidelity exude from every page, as does his awareness of the trends of our culture that need to be addressed if we are truly and correctly to see what Scripture teaches. Although this book is relatively short, it is packed! Readers will find excellent biblical exposition and incisive analysis that will inform their minds and inflame their hearts. Among other reactions to this book, Christian readers in particular will find ample reason here for increased humility, reverence, and worship as they reflect on the horror God has spared them from, along with the endless joy He is preparing them to know. It is arguable that nothing in this life now matters more than knowing what happens then. And, of course, this includes knowing how to escape God's final judgment and enter God's everlasting life. I heartily hope and pray readers will not only grow in their understanding of Heaven and Hell from this book, but that they will see more clearly the reasons God has so designed the world to end in this way. For His glory, and for the good of those who contemplate and embrace (perhaps in time) the argument of this book, may these things be so.

Bruce A. Ware
Professor of Christian Theology
The Southern Baptist Theological Seminary Louisville,
Kentucky, USA

INTRODUCTION

If you have picked this book up and are looking for a story of someone who has been to either Heaven or to Hell, you will be disappointed. If you are reading it with the hopes of learning something about the life to come, you are wasting your time as well.

I find books and stories about people who claim to have died and gone to Heaven or Hell to be bizarre and unconvincing.

To begin with, I do not believe they died. Typically, medical experts will define death as either the irreversible cessation of circulatory and respiratory functions, or the irreversible cessation of the functions of the entire brain, including the stem. In laymen's terms, this means that either the heart or the brain has permanently ceased to function. The important phrase is "permanent cessation" — that is, death.

People who make claims to have been to the other side and can now report back what they witnessed were never dead. Some people have experienced the cessation of a heartbeat only to have been saved from death through heroic medical intervention. But these people most certainly did not die. Vital functions were temporarily halted and the body was put into distress. It is accurate to say they *came close* to dying, but it is simply false to claim they died and came back. Medical professionals don't talk about people dying and coming back to life, so we too should be deeply suspicious when people attempt to market an account of what happens after death.

Let's assume the stories we have in mind are not of death, but of people who came close to it. We must then admit there are many other stories of people claiming a near-death experience. Typically, these will include the experience of the person feeling themselves floating above their own body and looking down. Some claim to have experienced meeting people, angels, or other beings in another realm. Some people with no religion of any sort have reported feeling incredible love and acceptance in the realm they found themselves in. They claimed that the experience made them unafraid of death. And some religious folks have claimed to have gone to Heaven. Some have even said they met God, who gave them a message to share with us still in the realm of the living. One wonders if God decided He hadn't said everything He wanted to say in the Bible, and was now adding a few extra thoughts.

Since these experiences are many and varied, we are left to theorize about them. Are we to assume they are all fraudulent? Perhaps, but not necessarily. One common explanation is that those in great physical distress experience hallucinations of their oxygen-starved and potentially dying brain. This is possible. If this explanation is accepted, we might also argue for two other things. First, as is true in all hallucinations, those experiences are not to be thought of as existing in reality. Second, we would have to assume that the person's ability to accurately recall the experience is questionable. We would also have to ask, "Why would having emergency surgery or experiencing severe bodily distress usher one into Heaven for a short period of time?" There is no reason for believing it would.

Therefore, if the experience was a hallucination, we should also assume that the person's pre-existing worldview would interpret their near-death experience in line with what they already believed. Those who are religious would interpret their experience through their doctrinal grid, and those who are non-religious would interpret theirs through their own worldview. If this is what occurred, it would explain why the religious are more likely to claim to see God and the non-religious are more likely to claim to see friends or perhaps beings from another dimension.

Others insist that these experiences tell us that we have a soul that continues to live, even after it appears the body is dying. In some cases they argue that the person is having an out-of-body experience. Some even claim to have seen things in the operating theatre even though they were unconscious at the time. Is it possible that people really do have experiences of their souls hovering over their physical selves? Does the soul, in times of severe physical crisis, slip out of the body?

If this is the case, we must also conclude that such experiences are not restricted to those who are in danger of dying. Numerous forms of spiritualities claim they can mimic that experience during meditation. Others claim it can be accomplished in a drug-induced state. Still, even if these are real experiences, experts are divided on their nature. Many in healthcare see such out-of-body experiences as a pathological condition that involves the seeing of a second self. That is, these experiences are a fracturing of the psyche. They are the first stages of what might become a complete mental collapse. Faced with the prospect of dying, the mind is put into severe distress.

I raise all these issues not to resolve them, but to point out that there is nothing definitive about any of the purported experiences coming from individuals who claim to have been to the other side and come back. For one, the stories can't be verified. Furthermore, these experiences, if they are real, can be explained in a variety of ways. At this time we can safely say that nothing definitive can be ascertained from these many and varied experiences. The discerning reader should take all the books that claim such experiences with a very large grain of salt.

Confessional Christians do not believe in Heaven and Hell because of subjective human experiences. Whatever their confusing nature, none of them offer us an objective insight into what awaits us beyond the grave.

This book discusses what the Bible teaches about death and the life to come, but the skeptic might respond by asking whether the Bible's teaching isn't also derived from a human perspective. Doesn't the Bible build the case for life after death from the experiences people have had with the subject?

My answer to that question is a firm no. Nothing of what the Bible teaches about the life to come has anything to do with the experiences of those who have been near death or died.

In contrast, the Bible tells us of a number of cases of people dying who were raised to life. In these cases there was indeed a permanent cessation. Furthermore, in some cases the body had begun to decompose. But not so with any of the many contemporary accounts that have been popularized in our day.

There are several examples in the Bible of people who were raised from the dead. 1 Kings 17 recounts the story of a widow from the town of Zarephath, in the region of ancient Tyre. Her son died and the prophet Elijah raised him from the dead. 2 Kings 4 recounts the story of a boy from the town of Shunem in Israel who died. Elisha, the disciple of Elijah, raised him from the dead. 2 Kings 13 tells of a dead man who was thrown into the grave of Elisha; he revived and stood to his feet.

Jesus was said to have raised three people from the dead: the son of the widow from Nain (Luke 7), the daughter of Jairus (Luke 8), and Jesus's friend Lazarus (John 11). In the account of Lazarus, the body was already placed into a tomb and had begun to decompose, so much so that the odour of death was overwhelming.

There are two examples of the raising of the dead found after the time of Jesus. in Acts 9, Peter raises a woman named Tabitha, and in Acts 20, Paul raises a man named Eutychus.

And so, quite apart from the resurrection of Jesus, which belongs in a category unlike the other accounts, we conclude that there have been times when the dead have actually come back to life. If this is the case, what can we learn about the life to come from these people?

None of the biblical accounts of the raising of the dead contain details about what the dead may have experienced in the afterlife. If these events had occurred today, we would no doubt have sent a reporter to interview them on precisely this question. Furthermore, many book publishers would be keen to offer up a contract for an exposé on that very issue. But the Bible does not satisfy our curiosity as to what the dead experienced. John 12 says a large crowd gathered in the home of Lazarus—but the crowd is there to meet Jesus. They are fascinated to know more about His power to raise the dead. They look to Lazarus not to tell of his experience in the life beyond the grave, but to verify that he really was raised back to life. If you are looking for subjective accounts of the afterlife in the Bible, you will be disappointed.

What the Bible teaches about life after death are words of divine revelation. God has chosen to reveal something of the life to come. Even in the case of Jesus's stories of the deaths of a rich man and of another man named Lazarus, we are not given the privilege of interviewing them. They are now dead and beyond our ability to communicate with. But rather, since He is the Son of God, Jesus knows what became of them in the afterlife, and lets us know.

This is a book about the life to come, and it will argue that there are only two destinies that come into being after death: the one who has died either goes to Heaven or to Hell. The reason for this claim is none other than the fact that the Bible makes it.

How then can we think meaningfully on Heaven and Hell without resorting to flights of fancy or unprovable assumptions? The answer begins with the understanding that the Bible is the inerrant, authoritative word of God, and has much to say about both Heaven and Hell. People are often surprised to hear that Jesus spoke more on the subject than anyone else in scripture. Furthermore, His word is to be considered, for not only does He claim to be Lord of Heaven and Hell, but He also died and rose again.

And so, if in picking up this book about Heaven and Hell you thought you would read the next titillating account of someone who claimed to have visited one or both of those places, you will be sadly disappointed. But if you press on and continue to read, you will be surprised to find that the Bible paints a far more fascinating picture of the afterlife than any one of the subjective accounts that have become so very popular.

CHAPTER ONE

THE REALITY OF DEATH

For the young and healthy, the subject of Heaven and Hell can seem futuristic, on a distant horizon. For the old, one would think it a different matter, yet I have found that this is not always the case. I have engaged in numerous conversations with people in their eighties who testify they never think about death. There are reasons for this. Many North Americans have never witnessed anyone dying, nor have they seen a dead body. We no longer speak about funerals; rather, we have a "celebration of life." Wearing clothing that reflects mourning and the practice of weeping is often not on display. The body is not observed, for we think that to be macabre. It is now common for there to be no memorial service at all.

People might discuss "death with dignity." By that they mean they want to die on their own terms, before they are faced with crippling pain or hopelessness, but the actual subject of death and the events that attend its experience are seldom addressed. It is to this reality that we begin our study.

There are two fixed points in our lives: birth and death. The subject of our death may seem uncomfortable. Some even argue that it is preferable never to think about it. Why not live life to the fullest, thinking only about life? Doesn't thinking about death simply make us morbid? Shouldn't our experiences in life be our focus of concern? And so, armed with this perspective, we put death out of our minds.

On the other hand, there are others (I among them) who think about death every single day. Richard Baxter, an English Puritan preacher in the 1600s, said he preached every sermon as if it was his last, to a congregation who has no assurance that they would ever hear another.[1] As Baxter looked out to his congregation, he did not think they were guaranteed to be there even in the following week. Nor did he think he had any assurance that he would be there either. From his perspective, this great certainty of death put urgency into every message he preached.

The great American preacher and theologian Jonathan Edwards devised a list of resolutions that he read to himself every day. He intended this list to be a stable anchor to direct his daily life. One of his resolutions included these words: "Resolved, to think much, on all occasions, of my dying, and of the common circumstances which attend death."[2] He believed this daily thinking about death would bring focus to his life. And so, Edwards never allowed a day to pass in which he did not fix his thoughts on the certainty of his own death. This resolve might explain why it was, when he suddenly became ill because of an improper dose of the smallpox vaccine, that he didn't struggle. He had prepared himself for that moment through much of his life. In peace he embraced the day he had been anticipating.

---

[1] *The Poetical Fragments of Richard Baxter*, Richard Baxter, 1821
[2] *The Works of Jonathan Edwards (Vol 1)*, Jonathan Edwards. Banner of Truth Trust, 1974

Thinking about our own mortality: What Moses can teach us

How are we to think about our own death? A good place to start would be to consider the words of Psalm 90. This is the only psalm of the 150 in the Bible that was written by Moses.

This fact has led many Bible teachers to wonder at what significant moment Moses might have written Psalm 90. Some have suggested that the background is Numbers 13–14, which is the account of what happened at Kadesh Barnea. It was here that Israel rebelled against God out of fear of being destroyed by the powerful warriors of Canaan. Israel was then standing at the threshold of the Promised Land. Spies had been sent in to gain all the information they could. They returned with both a hopeful and a fearful response. Yes, the land was as beautiful and fruitful as God had promised it would be. But the inhabitants of the land were powerful. Ten of the twelve spies counselled turning back. "If we enter the land, we will all fall by the sword," they said. "Our children will be massacred." And so, with a lack of trust in the promises God had made to them, and out of fear of death, they turned back.

Consequently, an entire generation was condemned to wander in a hostile desert for forty years. God had indicated that the entire generation of adults who refused His commands would not enter the Promised Land. They would die in the desert. Over the next forty years, Moses watched two million people die. It was, if you will, the world's longest funeral march. He would have witnessed, on average, 50,000 funerals every year. That would have been over a hundred a day. No wonder Moses thought much of death and the brevity of life.

Psalm 90 doesn't tell us that it was written with the events of Kadesh Barnea in mind. Others suggest Moses wrote this Psalm coinciding with the events in Numbers 20, which was immediately after the death of Miriam, his sister. Still others suggest that he may have written this poem after his own sin, when he himself did not fully obey God. In consequence, God forbade him from entering the Promised Land. The outcome would have been plain to Moses. He would join the two-million-person funeral march. He would not be exempt from the fate of the rest of his generation. Still others wonder if Psalm 90 was written after the death of his brother Aaron.

The point is that there were many occasions in Moses's life that might have given rise to Psalm 90. The man who wrote it had become intimate with death. It was constantly around him. He would have, in consequence of his own experience, been forced to think about death and the common events that surrounded the expiry of human beings. Whatever the occasion for the writing of Psalm 90, one matter remains clear: Moses lived in the valley of the shadow of death.

Moses was not just a man who had seen his fair share of deaths. He was also a man who had come to see that life is so very short. Witnessing death and observing the brevity of all human life had left a significant impact. What is remarkable about Psalm 90, however, is Moses's attitude towards death. Old Testament scholar H. C. Leupold observes, "There does not appear to be any trace of bitterness or of undue pessimism [about death]. Just plain, realistic thinking marks these words."[3]

Psalm 90 is not a poem of despair. Moses is not shaking his fist at death. Nor is he shaking in fear and desperation before it. Rather, Moses is merely considering that which is plain to anyone who takes the time to notice: we are all dying! This is the universal reality.

A moment's reflection tells us that we all share in Moses's experience. Think about it in terms of our contemporary experience. Roughly speaking, about 150,000 people die globally

---

[3] *Expositions of Psalms*, Herbert C. Leupold. Baker Publishing Group, 1970

every day. That would be the population of Sherbrooke, Quebec, or Hollywood, California, dying daily. Every week the equivalent of Phoenix, Arizona, dies. Every year a rough equivalent of the United Kingdom simply disappears from the earth and is never seen again.

Consequently, the planet has never known a time when people are not in mourning. Many will wail inconsolably and be crushed in anguish. The cries of despair and defeat that rise from this planet every day are almost deafening. It is amazing that many never think about it. How blind can we be to the greatest event on earth? It is a trauma that stalks us. While we may not notice it, Moses did.

Our study begins with the first four verses of Psalm 90:

> Lord, you have been our dwelling place in all generations. Before the mountains were brought forth, or ever you had formed the earth and the world, from everlasting to everlasting you are God. You return man to dust and say, "Return, O children of man!" For a thousand years in your sight are but as yesterday when it is past, or as a watch in the night.

We are a moment, God is eternal

Moses saw the reality of the human condition: we are all facing death. He saw that God is eternal. He also saw that we are momentary. This perspective is essential as we consider our own death.

Moses describes God as being from everlasting to everlasting. He means that if we were able to go backwards into a distant time, we would never find an age when God was not there. But if we were to go forward into an infinite future, we would also never find a time when God is not there. He is the everlasting God.

Moses then contrasts that with our own existence. The first word that comes to his mind is "dust." Moses wrote the book of Genesis, and there in Chapter 2 he describes man as created from the dust of the ground. But in Psalm 90, he speaks of returning to it. The cycle is complete. When we consider our own death, it must be in terms of our finite and temporary nature. We have no power to control this reality.

Hence, if we repeat our imaginary journey and go to a distant time in the past, we would find, unlike God, that we were not there. And if we project just a few short years in the future, we see that we are not there either. We are reminded of 1 Peter 1:24-25: "All flesh is like grass and all its glory like the flower of grass. The grass withers, and the flower falls, but the word of the Lord remains forever." Or we might meditate on James 1:11: "For the sun rises with its scorching heat and withers the grass; its flower falls, and its beauty perishes. So also, will the rich man fade away in the midst of his pursuits." We might even consider Jesus's parable in Luke 12. A man was making his economic plans. He had a terrific formula. He would build bigger barns and take on massive projects. But then came a word from God: "This night your soul is required of you." Suddenly all plans came to an end. In none of them did this man consider the reality of death. He may have thought he could control his life and death, but he was deluded. How foolish he was. Why did he make plans without considering the only thing that was a certainty?

Many of us may think the goal is to avoid death. But long lives only postpone death, they do not avoid it. When Moses mentions the significance of time, he says that a thousand years in God's sight are but as yesterday when it is past. Some have suggested that when he speaks of a thousand years, he is speaking of the longest lifespan the human race has seen.

Remember that Moses is the author of Genesis. Genesis 5:27 says, "Thus all the days of Methuselah were 969 years, and he died." To us, this lifespan seems nothing short of incredible. If we lived as Methuselah did, our hundredth birthday would seem but the beginning of our adventure of life. We would look forward to a long and enduring future.

And yet, Methuselah himself is not remembered for anything other than that he lived 969 years, and then he died. What he did, what he loved, what he hated, what he accomplished, where he went, and what he succeeded and failed in has been swept away like dust. It is no more. Many thousands of years have come and gone since his long life.

In God's sight, Methuselah's life is like a watch in the night. A night watch for a guard in an ancient city would typically last for three hours. The ancients realized that staring into the blackness in the most vulnerable part of a day was tiring work. If one left a watchman for too long, it is quite likely that he would become inattentive, giving an attacker a formidable advantage. To counter this, night watches were shortened. And that is Moses's point on long lives. Against the eternal perspective, even Methuselah's life is but a moment.

Psalm 90:5–6 gives three images that help us picture the brevity of life: "You sweep them away as with a flood; they are like a dream, like grass that is renewed in the morning: in the morning it flourishes and is renewed; in the evening it fades and withers."

Since Moses would have written Psalm 90 while in the wilderness of Sinai, we have to imagine he had seen a flash flood. These are often the result of rain being experienced in another location. Because of the nature of desert soil, the rain cannot penetrate it. The water rushes along the hardened soil, finding the lowest point of land. From the perspective of a human, the flood comes without warning. It may seem to be a day like so many others: no difficulties are expected. Who knew that it had rained somewhere far away? But suddenly the waters of a flood are all around and there is no escaping its fury. Death is sometimes like that. I have seen even the elderly shocked when the day of their death came upon them. But even when it is expected, the fury of death is often greater than anticipated.

The second image Moses uses is that of a dream. Dreams can be vivid while they are being experienced, but when we awake in the morning, the memory of the dream is quickly forgotten. This is an enigma to many. How can something that seems so memorable be gone within a few minutes of waking? And yet, says Moses, so are our lives. Suddenly we are gone, and we are not remembered.

Think of the many obituaries written in newspapers: "Never forgotten," they say, "always remembered." What is left unsaid is that the people who are determined not to forget the deceased will soon also be forgotten. Like a dream, we are soon forgotten.

I have often talked with elderly people on their birthdays. They always tell me two things. First, they are amazed that they have lived so long, but second, they are amazed how quickly that time is gone. This is the universal testimony of the elderly. And so, like Moses, they see that God is eternal and we are a moment. This is the perspective we must bear in mind as we consider our own death.

Our comfort in death

While this may sound depressingly morbid to us, Moses said it is possible to take comfort in our mortality and God's eternity.

What is fascinating in Psalm 90 is not just the contrast that Moses gives us between God's eternal being and our momentary existence, but rather how he responds to this. Look again at verse 1: "Lord, you have been our dwelling place in all our generations."

Imagine Moses as the man who has no dwelling place. He has left Egypt with two million people. Numbers 33 records all of Israel's campsites on the way to the Promised Land. Between Rameses in Egypt and the plains of Moab, which is on the edge of the Promised Land, there were forty different camps. In other words, in forty years they moved forty times!

If you moved forty times in forty years, you would have difficulty calling any place home. But Moses says, "God has been my home." The one constant in an everchanging world has been his God. He never changes. His promises never fail.

We might want to consider the contrast between God and ourselves as we think about our own lives and mortality. Our environment changes, our job changes, people close to us die, but God is ever constant. We need to be aware of God's presence and constantly remind ourselves that He is the only constant in our life. He is our true dwelling place.

Given what has been said, we might think Moses would continue in that comforting theme. But what he says next may surprise us: "For we are brought to an end by your anger; by your wrath we are dismayed. You have set our iniquities before you, our secret sins in the light of your presence. For all our days pass away under your wrath; we bring our years to an end like a sigh" (Psalm 90:7–9).

We might have expected something a little more encouraging than this. For instance, why not say, "The hard things were possible because God was my dwelling place"? Instead, Moses argues that God is angry with us and is putting all of us to death. It is important to understand why Moses speaks this way. That was his experience. The generation that sinned against God in Kadesh Barnea was condemned by God to die in that desolate, howling wasteland in the Sinai Peninsula. Their children would see the Promised Land, but they who had sinned were condemned to die there.

In truth, though, I don't think Moses was referring to that. In Genesis 3, Moses traced death to the sin of Adam. God told him that the day he ate of the forbidden fruit, defying God's command, would be the day he would die. Adam died, and so did all of his descendants. Moses was completely aware that sin causes death. For Moses, what happened at Kadesh Barnea was merely a further extension of the Adamic sin and its consequences.

You will notice, however, that he does more than simply repeat a theological theme. That is, Moses says more than that death reigned in the human race from Adam onward. Rather, Moses makes it personal. Verse 8 speaks about secret sins, and verse 9 speaks about God's response in wrath. Finally, we are told that all of us end this life with a sigh.

So, how does God deal with the sin of the human race? He causes every person who sins to die. We are all like prisoners on death row. We are awaiting the day when our sentence is justly carried out.

New Testament believers know that Christ died for us and that He bore the wrath of the Father in His own body. Why then do Christians die? Do we also die because of sin and wrath? And if we do, what does that say about what Christ accomplished? Has He not taken the punishment of our sins from us? And if we don't die because of our sins, why do we often suffer and die, just like anyone else? What can be the answer to this conundrum?

Christians die, but not because of sin. Christ died for us, and hence the penalty for our sin has fallen on Him. And yet we find that we still die. What is to account for this? We perish to identify with Christ when we die. God graciously allows us a union with Christ, even in His death. But those who have no claim to Christ die because of God's anger for their sins.

Moses adds a further thought. In Psalm 90:10 he says, "The years of our life are seventy, or even by reason of strength eighty, yet their span is but toil and trouble; they are soon gone, and we fly away."

And so, says Moses, none of us will avoid toil and trouble. And none of us will avoid flying away when our time comes. The news around the world is this: the mortality rate is still 100 percent.

The truth of the mortality rate leads Moses to ask us an important question: "Who considers the power of your anger, and your wrath according to the fear of you?" (Psalm 90:11). In asking that question, Moses clearly indicates to us what our attitude toward death really should be. We need to be overwhelmed by the determined justice of God. We will not escape His righteous anger toward our sin. Fear is an appropriate response.

Let's remember what it is we are considering: how powerful is God's anger? It is so powerful that he puts 55 million people to death every year. Eventually He will put to death every single one of the over seven billion human beings that populate the planet. Who considers this?

CHAPTER TWO

COMING TO TERMS WITH HEAVEN AND HELL

Preparing for a journey

I once had a conversation about life and death with an old friend. Through a long series of events, he had gone from being an atheist to becoming fairly convinced there was a God. That was a good start, but there was so much further to go. He was on a journey. He had also recently become convinced that Jesus was probably the Son of God. And yet there was still a distance to go. Still, I was overjoyed at the progress he was making. The trajectory showed me he was going in the right direction.

Somehow our conversations moved to the subject of the afterlife. My old friend told me he had no reason for believing he would survive his own death. He said, "If there is life after death, I guess I'll find out then." In a way, that made sense. The idea of a Heaven and a Hell seemed like mere speculation to him. He said that no one has ever gone to the other side and come back, reporting what awaits us there. As he saw it, even if someone were to make that claim, there was no objective way to examine it. It was not possible to investigate the matter. On that basis, he thought, one needed to live one's life with a moral compass pointed towards God. This was the best that one could do. Should there be a judgment at the end of it all, a moral life would stand one in good stead—speculation about the afterlife was to no advantage.

I said to him that I had never known anyone who took a journey from which they were never to return who did not make some inquiry about what awaited them. I imagined a person going from North America to Europe, intent on living the rest of their life there. Wouldn't they want to know something about what awaited them on the other side of the ocean? What language is spoken? What customs are observed? What kinds of houses are lived in? How are relationships maintained? What is the cost of living? What jobs are in high demand, and will finding work be difficult?

I asked him, "Doesn't everyone inquire about what will greet them when they are about to take a journey from which they will not return?" The wise always plan. And in the case of death, would it not be wise to know what awaits us? For we will not return. The answer to our inquiry will lead us to think carefully about how we lead our lives today. If nothing awaits us, then all the decisions we make now are inconsequential for the afterlife. Then let us eat and drink, for tomorrow we die. But if something awaits us, a cavalier attitude about this world's decisions is foolhardy. Indeed, are we not right to spend a great deal of time and energy investigating what evidence there might be for a journey after death?

He agreed. But still, he said, "How can we know if there are preparations to be made? If death is the extinction of all consciousness, no preparations are required. But even if another land awaits us, how do we prepare for the unknown?" The great irony of the ancient Pharaohs is that they prepared for the afterlife by being sealed into their tombs with the things that would be required in the life to come. And yet, those things were stolen by grave robbers. In the end, the only use of all those things was that they were again used in this life, and not the one to come. How foolish it would be to prepare for the life to come based upon faulty evidence leading to faulty reasoning.

I said, "The Bible provides the reader with a travel brochure to the next life. If the Bible comes from God, then it is imperative to learn all we can about what awaits us." Again, he agreed. Our conversations continued. The importance of knowing whether the Bible is the Word of God became critical.

The pervasiveness of belief in the afterlife

The reason I recount this conversation is that the belief that death is the cessation of existence continues only among a minority of the earth's population. All cultures of the earth have a history of believing in a life that follows this one. Buddhism and Hinduism speak of reincarnation, or the transmigration of souls into different bodies. But for both religions, the goal is to escape the cycle of endless death and rebirth. Buddhists hope for Nirvana, and Hindus hope to return to be with Brahman. In either case, the goal is to escape personal consciousness and be swallowed up into the one reality, forever losing individual identity. In some ways, this belief of the eventual ending of individual existence is close to the atheistic belief of the end of personal consciousness. Still, both Buddhists and Hindus affirm life beyond the grave.

There are other views as well. Spiritualists think of an afterworld in which souls evolve and continue to interact with the living through mediums. From their perspective, the life to come has a great deal of continuity with the present one. The ancient Greeks and Romans believed in the underworld and its god. Greeks tended to believe that the body was the prison-house for the soul. It was necessary, therefore, that one escape earthly attachments, lest the soul not be able to break with the body.

They were not alone in their understanding of a realm of the dead that included conscious existence. Whether it be the First Peoples of North America, the Aztecs, ancient people from India, the Celts, the Etruscans, or the Romans, afterlife beliefs are held in every culture on earth. If the matter of an afterlife is as tenuous as the Western naturalist believes it to be, why is its belief so globally persistent? Furthermore, not only do all cultures hold to an afterlife, but they believe that the things that are done in this life have a bearing on what is experienced in the life to come.

Western naturalists must despair that survey after survey finds that, by far, the majority of North Americans not only believe in an afterlife, but also in Heaven. Indeed, far more North Americans believe in Heaven than in God. They believe that there will be a continuation of existence after death, and that the life to come will be pleasant and delightful. And almost all who believe in a Heaven think they are going to go there. Because most North Americans have a low consciousness of sin, the idea of personal guilt that would disqualify them from Heaven seems like an unrealistic danger. Most who do believe in Hell simply assume it is reserved only for the world's most monstrous villains.

Why does everyone hope for an afterlife?

There are several possible explanations for the pervasive belief in an afterlife. Some might argue that superstition is the explanation. But why is it so enduring? Why such a global supra-cultural superstition?

Others might argue that this widely held belief is because of the human fear of death. Of course, it is true that all human beings harbour this dread. We were created to live, not to die. The fall of humanity into sin has introduced something that is unnatural into our being. Intuitively, we know we were created to live and not die, but the abhorrence of death does not necessitate the idea of an afterlife. Atheists, like the rest of humanity, also fear death. But I would argue that the reason they deny the afterlife is because they have a greater fear than death: they fear God and His judgment. And so, they imagine their owns myths in which an afterlife consists of nothing. In this way they escape the consequences of their misdeeds in life. Hence, to use fear as an explanation of afterlife beliefs is a sword that cuts both ways. It can just as easily describe naturalism/atheism as it can the person who believes that something awaits us after the grave.

The more plausible explanation of the persistence of afterlife beliefs is that this is part of what it means to be in the image of God. We were created with eternity in view. Ecclesiastes 3:11 says that God has placed eternity into the hearts of every human being. We will never outgrow the desire for eternity and the sense that it lies before us. Eternity is deeply rooted into the human consciousness. This, then, is the explanation for the enduring belief in an afterlife.

Can we have confidence in Heaven?

In Psalm 90, we notice several things. First, Moses witnessed much death. Furthermore, he was a nomad. For him, the belief that he had no permanent dwelling on earth was one he would have easily embraced. His hope was that the Lord was his dwelling place.

We also notice that Moses places a great deal of emphasis on the fact that, while God is altogether everlasting, we are not. Our lifespan is but a moment in time, and soon we are no more. In Moses's own words, "The years of our life are seventy, or even by reason of strength eighty; yet their span is but toil and trouble; they are soon gone, and we fly away" (Psalm 90:10).

But then we also notice that Moses states that, "We are brought to an end by your anger; by your wrath we are dismayed. You have set our iniquities before you, our secret sins in the light of your presence. For all our days pass away under your wrath" (Psalm 90: 7–9).

For Moses, the reason for death is twofold. First was the issue of sin. By that, Moses meant we have all broken God's divine law, and in response he thought that God was angry. Second, in His anger it was God, not natural forces, that subjected all of humanity to death. The reason we die, said Moses, is that God is provoked because of human sin. Were it not for the fact that we had violated divine law, we would not be facing death. We would continue to live. It was Moses who wrote the words from Genesis 2 indicating that, on the day our first parents ate from the tree of good and evil, they would surely die.

We are left then with only a few conclusions regarding the cataclysm of the great company of men and women who die every day. Either God is simply watching but unconcerned with this appalling catastrophe, or God—in His anger, as Moses said—is putting people to death. If Moses is right, God is presently planning to put to death every one of the billions of people alive today, so that in a few short years not one of us remains.

The Bible's own testimony is that Moses is right. God brings us to an end in His anger so that we end our years with a sigh. But for those who disagree, who think that God is merely allowing all of us to die, where does this confidence that we are all going to Heaven come from? If God is not saving humans from death right now, but is allowing this unrelenting highway of carrion, then we must consider the question asked by Moses, "Who considers the power of your anger, and your wrath according to the fear of you?" (Psalm 90:11).

Moses invites us to consider the all-important question, "Are you overwhelmed by the power of God?" If you are not, you are a fool! Psalm 90:11 is a rhetorical question. The answer is that no one is overwhelmed by the power and wrath of God. That seems unbelievable. When we think about it, the groans, the cries of anguish, the weeping, and the daily sadness of humanity are overwhelming. Death is the major issue facing people.

Feeling a bit morbid and depressed? Wondering how you will answer when someone asks you if you believe in Heaven and Hell? Let me suggest two prayers for those who dare to ponder the power of God.

Prayer #1: Dear Lord, I need perspective on my life

Psalm 90:12 says, "So teach us to number our days that we may get a heart of wisdom." The idea of numbering our days may seem foreign to us. If you knew you had a hundred days left to live, and you thought about it, you might wake up tomorrow and say, "I have 99 days left." On the next day, you would say you had 98. And as the number got smaller, every day you would become much more sober in your assessment about how you might want to think about each day and the value you place on it.

Of course, most of us don't know how many days we have. According to Hebrews 9:27, our death is according to the appointment of God. God has your death day written in His day-timer and you will die right on His schedule, even though you work out, eat bean sprouts, and stay gluten-free.

Prayer #2: Dear Lord, treat me as an object of your mercy

Psalm 90:13 says, "Return, O LORD! How long? Have pity on your servants!" Notice the word *servants*. Moses sees himself not as a rebel to God, but as one who is created to serve him. As one who willingly bends the knee to God, he is mindful he is not deserving of God's blessing. So, he asks that God treat him with pity.

Every one of us should pray as follows: "Have pity on me, oh God, and treat me with mercy and not as my sins deserve. Having considered the power of Your anger and having been allowed to see that all human death is related to Your anger, what can I do but appeal to You for mercy?"

As Moses would see it, Heaven is not a default position. He does not assume we are all going there unless we do something profoundly evil. Rather, he believes that the reality of death tells us that we have already done something profoundly evil. Indeed, God is provoked and is putting us to death. Our only response must be to cry out to Him for mercy.

If the Bible's testimony is to be believed, Heaven is not assured. Rather, Heaven is given as a gift of God's grace despite our sins. That's why, before we talk about Heaven, we need to talk about how we can get there.

In Randy Alcorn's book on Heaven,[4] he cites a *Los Angeles Times* survey in which, for every one person who believes they are going to Hell, there are 120 who believe they are going to Heaven. Yet in Matthew 7:13–14, Jesus said, "Enter by the narrow gate. For the gate is wide and the way is easy that leads to destruction, and those who enter by it are many. For the gate is narrow and the way is hard that leads to life, and those who find it are few." According to Jesus, the majority are going to Hell and not Heaven. And that assertion accords perfectly with Moses's thoughts in Psalm 90.

According to the Bible, not only is Heaven real, but so is Hell. And should we decide to move beyond the fairy-tale Jesus of human imagination and read the real eye-witness accounts of the real Jesus, we will be shocked to find out how many

---

[4] *Heaven*, Randy Alcorn. Carol Stream, IL: Tyndale House Publishers, 2004

times He spoke about and warned about Hell. He called it the "Hell of fire." He often warned about the dangers of going there. In Matthew 10:28, He warned us to fear God—the God who, in Jesus's words, has the power to destroy both body and soul in Hell. Indeed, in Luke 12 Jesus even said that God has the authority to throw us into Hell. He said, "If your right eye causes you to sin, pluck it out, for it would be better to lose an eye than to go to Hell where suffering never ends." All of us should hear that there is but one basis upon which pity can be found. Since God is not only gracious but just, justice must be satisfied. And it was: 2000 years ago, Christ was brutally tortured to death on a cross. While hanging on that cross, He drank the full cup of the Father's righteous anger for the sins of the whole world. According to Romans 4:5, He did so in order that anyone who believes in Him who justifies the ungodly would be counted as righteous.

Let me put that simply: if you will turn from your love of sin and sinning; if you will confess your sins and repent of them; if you will turn to Christ and believe that His horrifying death on the cross satisfied God's desire for justice; and if you surrender your life, your future, and your way of life into His hands, you will find that your name has been written in the Book of Life. That is where mercy is found.

Of course, all of that is more than what Moses said. Moses lived before Christ, and he simply believed he needed mercy. But because of Christ we now know where mercy is to be found. But do not be deceived. Heaven is not the default destination, Hell is.

Many an unwise person has taken their eyes off the ball and forgotten about death, God, the judgment to come, and the reality of their need for mercy. Indeed, they haven't attained perspective on the reality of their own death, and that we are (as Peter told us) like grass. Many of us have allowed ourselves to become sidetracked in the things that don't count for eternity, and we have never considered the power of God's anger. We carefully consider the matter of careers, love, goals in life, and plans to see the world and retirement opportunities, but we neglect the matter of our eternal destiny. And without any wisdom at all, we have merely assumed we are going to Heaven. We have lived a life of illusion. If that describes you, consider that you have but a short amount of time remaining. But don't despair as you do so. Rather, come to God for mercy.

CHAPTER THREE

THINKING THE UNTHINKABLE

If you have never heard or read an extended teaching on Hell, I suspect the realities of what you learn will leave you more horrified than you have ever been in your life. If you have been entertained by movies that depict Hell in less than biblical terms, you will be shocked to find that those movies were a great deal milder than the real thing. Hell is not the subject of entertainment. Neither is it the fitting subject of crude jesting. It must never be used as a curse. The reality is too awful for such nonsense.

Furthermore, if you have never heard or read an extended teaching on Hell, you will be amazed that this reality has never been explained to you. Hell is so horrifying that the Doctrine of Hell leaves some angry. Others become despondent or deeply shocked that this doctrine is found in our Bible, and still others are overwhelmed by terror. Still others wonder if they have ever understood God at all.

Let us then address the obvious question: why conduct a study on Hell? What is it we would hope to accomplish by contemplating such awful subject matter? Let's consider three reasons for doing so.

1. Many have only a superficial understanding of Hell

Many contemporary believers have never heard a sermon about Hell or read a book on it. For the most part they are ignorant of the Doctrine of Hell, or the reason for its importance.

Often the existence of Hell is assumed but unspoken. After all, who would wish to consider the unthinkable? Frequently, one hears people saying, "The last thing we need is another hellfire-and-brimstone preacher or sermon." To that, I always respond, "When was the last time you heard a hellfire sermon?" Almost everyone I have spoken with agrees they have never heard one in their lives. Since so few have received formal instruction about this doctrine, we can expect that it would eventually be abandoned or substantially changed to no longer look like the biblical doctrine.

Recent years have seen much controversy regarding Hell. It is often denied. Others argue that it is of a limited duration. Surely it can't be eternal! That is too cruel to imagine! Still others argue that it is possible to be redeemed from Hell. There must be hope, even in Hell. Others argue that all the biblical language used to describe it is merely metaphorical. Surely the biblical language can't be taken literally!

This change from the historical Christian Doctrine of Hell is made possible in the light of the absence of clear teaching. When, in one generation, the topic of Hell is no longer the subject of our reading and study, or the topic of many sermons, it is often abandoned in the next generation. After all, the critics say, "How can we believe in a God who is a torturer?"

Consider the reality. It is now commonly believed that we must not use the topic to frighten people, or to threaten them. They must be drawn only by love, never by warnings of a great cataclysm ahead. Furthermore, if anyone does come to Christ through a fear of the danger that lies ahead, in many cases their conversion is held in question. Reacting in fear is seen as the antithesis of reacting out of love. How strange then to find the writer of Hebrews warning about the fearful expectation of judgment and the fury of fire that will consume the adversaries (Hebrews 10:27). Why does the Bible seem so at odds with contemporary reasoning?

Of course, we should and must stress the mercy, kindness, and love of God. We are to revel in the glory of these truths and teach them with great joy. God is merciful, loving, and kind. Oh, what glorious news! But Romans 2:4 teaches us that we must not presume upon the riches of God's kindness. It imagines an individual who sins wantonly and finds that God has not responded by meting out punishment. He therefore assumes that God is tolerant of his sin. After all, he continues to enjoy the good things in life, just as the man who endeavours to live in submission to God. God seems to be paying no attention at all.

But Romans 2:4 rightly explains what it is he is experiencing. God is not tolerant of wickedness. Judgment truly awaits the unrighteous. But, out of His forbearance, God is extending a season of kindness, allowing for a turning from sin and an appeal to God for mercy. Hence, even the kindness of God is reason to take warning! It will not go on forever.

Did Jesus use Hell as a tool to frighten people into repentance? Shockingly, He frequently did. Jesus said to the Jews in Capernaum, "I tell you, many will come from east and west and recline at table with Abraham, Isaac, and Jacob, in the kingdom of heaven, while the sons of the kingdom will be thrown into the outer darkness. In that place there will be weeping and gnashing of teeth" (Matthew 8:11–12).

If that sounds like a threat, it is. It was supposed to frighten the Jews living in Capernaum. Jesus often spoke of Hell to alarm people: "And do not fear those who kill the body but cannot kill the soul. Rather fear him who can destroy both soul and body in hell" (Matthew 10:28). Notice Jesus said you should fear God, who has the power to throw your soul and body into Hell.

Notice also that Jesus thought that those in Hell had been raised bodily, and thus were experiencing bodily torment. His hearers were in spiritual and physical danger.

We must consider this matter carefully. When, as some say, we should not frighten people with images of Hell, we betray that the way we think about things is diametrically opposed to the way Jesus thought about things.

Another objection one frequently hears is that preaching about Hell turns people away from the faith. Who could love a God like that? To that, we should make several observations. Yes, it is true that the caricature of the preacher who rubs his hands in glee as he depicts people suffering in Hell does offend people and turn them away. People suspect that such a preacher is no better than they are. He is not warning, he is condemning.

But warning people of the reality of Hell is not unloving. Let's consider a practical example. Do you object if you are told the risks of smoking? Does it seem unloving to be informed that cigarette smoking causes most cases of lung cancer? What if you are told that cigarette smoking has been directly linked to emphysema and chronic bronchitis, diseases that are a part of what is called chronic obstructive pulmonary disease? And what if you are told that smokers are twelve times more likely to die from these diseases than non-smokers? What if young men were told that smoking leads to sexual dysfunction? Does this information seem unloving? Of course not. To fail to tell of the dangers of smoking shows a callous disregard for others.

What if, while being told of the dangers that attend smoking, you were also told of programs that can help defeat nicotine addiction? Would you think the frightening language is just scaremongering and therefore unloving? No doubt some feel that way. While most of us agree that scaremongering by itself is not effective, we can also agree that showing the dangers ahead while providing safe and healthy alternatives is loving: it shows great concern.

If our culture didn't tell people the risks associated with smoking, it would be guilty of neglect and a callous lack of regard for people. Does it not, therefore, follow that if a church will not graciously and gently explain the Doctrine of Hell, what it is, and what causes people to go there, it is showing a callous lack of regard for the souls of its congregation?

Our motivation is important, but speaking about Hell is not incompatible with love. Failure to explain Hell is incompatible with love.

What should become of us when we no longer teach on this grave matter? Is the result not that the vast majority simply assume they will go to Heaven without having abandoned their sin, fleeing to Christ for mercy? Many have become accustomed to thinking about the subject of Hell as the stuff of jokes, and few now shudder at the horrifying reality of it. Clearly, this matter is not peripheral to our faith.

The consequences are felt everywhere. There is a lack of seriousness around our faith. Many of us do not fear sin. A great many of us do not fear God. And even more of us have no sense of the glory of the God, who so despises sin that He reserves Hell for those who will not repent. Furthermore, many of us can't even begin to conceive of a God who would send people there. Take away Hell from our language and in short order the entire nature of the faith changes.

2. We are lacking a proper motivation for missions

Without an understanding of the existence and Doctrine of Hell, missions will stall and people will perish. The nerve that has urged the church toward missions, evangelism, and giving up our lives for the witness of Jesus Christ has been based on an essential understanding of the reality of Hell and a desire to save people from perishing.

Hudson Taylor (1832–1905), for example, is considered one of the greatest missionaries in the history of the Baptist Church. The missiologist David Hesselgrave shows that Taylor himself said he would not have gone to China had he not believed that the Chinese people were lost on their way to Hell.[5] Amy Carmichael, one of the great Protestant missionaries who went to India, also affirmed that the reality of Hell proved to be motive for dedicating her life to missions.[6]

It should be said that all the greatest missionaries who began the modern world missions' movement—which has had a global impact and ushered millions upon millions into the Kingdom—believed in Hell. Although it would be wrong to say this was their only motivation, it would be equally wrong to say that Hell played only a small role in that motivation.

Michael Pocock writes:

> The biblical understanding of hell is fundamental to a Christian worldview and therefore cannot be neglected. The concept of "perishing" in John 3:16 . . . as interpreted in the context of other passages speaks of an eternity of suffering without God. The account of the rich man and Lazarus indicates continual pain . . . and Jesus' teaching of two destinies—eternal punishment and eternal life in Matthew 25:46 indicates that the reality of hell is a stimulus to pure living.[7]

---

[5] *Paradigms in Conflict: 15 Key Questions in Christian Missions Today,* David J. Hesselgrave and Keith Eitel. Grand Rapids, MI.: Kregal Academic and Professional, 2018

[6] *Amy Carmichael,* Janet and Geoff Benge. YWAM Publishing, 1998

[7] *The Changing Face of World Missions: Engaging Contemporary Issues and Trends,* Michael Pocock, Gailyn Van Rheenen, and Douglas McConnell. Baker Academic, 2009

We might add that, historically, it has been one of the central stimuli to the worldwide mission project.

So, let's refresh ourselves: why must we preach about, write about, and reflect on the reality of Hell? First, because most believers are, for the most part, ignorant of what the Doctrine of Hell is about. Second, the doctrine has been a vital part of the motivation for the advancement of the gospel.

3. We are missing Jesus's and the New Testament's understanding of Hell

Jesus referenced Hell frequently—any gospel that does not is one unlike that which was taught by Jesus.

Jesus says, "So it will be at the end of the age. The angels will come out and separate the evil from the righteous and throw them into the fiery furnace. In that place there will be weeping and gnashing of teeth" (Matthew 13:49–50).

Later, in Matthew 18:8–9, Jesus says, "And if your hand or your foot causes you to sin, cut it off and throw it away. It is better for you to enter life crippled or lame than with two hands or two feet to be thrown into the eternal fire. And if your eye causes you to sin, tear it out and throw it away. It is better for you to enter life with one eye than with two eyes to be thrown into the hell of fire."

Still further in Matthew 25:31–34, Jesus says, "When the Son of Man comes in his glory, and all the angels with him, then he will sit on his glorious throne. Before him will be gathered all the nations, and he will separate people one from another as a shepherd separates the sheep from the goats. And he will place the sheep on his right, but the goats on the left. Then the King will say to those on his right, 'Come, you who are blessed by my Father, inherit the kingdom prepared for you from the foundation of the world.'" And then later, in verse 41, He adds, "Then he will say to those on his left, 'Depart from me, you cursed, into the eternal fire prepared for the devil and his angels.'"

The Doctrine of Hell is not only frequently found in the teaching of Jesus, but it is also essential to the rest of the New Testament.

While Jesus mentioned the word "Hell" more frequently than we would find it mentioned in the Epistles, we find the *concept* of Hell mentioned frequently, even when the word is not used. Consider 2 Thessalonians 1:7-9, speaking of Christ's return: "When the Lord Jesus is revealed from heaven with his mighty angels in flaming fire, inflicting vengeance on those who do not know God and on those who do not obey the gospel of our Lord Jesus. They will suffer the punishment of eternal destruction, away from the presence of the Lord and from the glory of his might."

We need to take note of three surprising truths from 2 Thessalonians. First, we notice that it is Jesus himself who inflicts vengeance. Second, we must note that the punishment being threatened is not of a limited duration, but is eternal. Finally, we should bear in mind that the Thessalonian Church, who received Paul's letter, understood this teaching as basic to their Christian instruction. This was, apparently, what Paul taught every church.

In noticing the frequency of New Testament teaching concerning Hell, also consider Revelation 20:15, which says, "If anyone's name was not found written in the book of life, he was thrown into the lake of fire." Hence, the Doctrine of Hell is not taught only on occasion, but the matter comes up with such frequency that it must be considered essential to early Christian discipleship.

4. We are lacking a seriousness regarding this matter

"Do not be deceived," says Paul in 1 Corinthians 6:9. He is warning the Corinthian Church that the sexually immoral will not inherit the Kingdom of God. Regardless of what theology some of them might have believed, they needed to be corrected. You can't profess Christ and remain sexually immoral. Given that only one of two destinies awaits all of us, the reality of Hell ought to arrest our attention when we consider the temptation to live in sexual sin. If you continue to live in sexual sin without repentance, you will go to Hell.

Contrast Paul's serious warning with the common discovery of a Christian leader in a lifetime of adulterous sins. The lack of seriousness that attends the consequences of such sin is remarkable. What if, in contemplating adultery, the Christian leader were to say to himself, "If I do this, I will go to Hell." Of course, there can be repentance, but the hardness of hearts that often attends sexual sins can make repentance seem distant.

This then is one example of the outcomes of a lack of seriousness around the Doctrine of Hell, so few see Hell as a real possibility. Hence, they sin with ease.

What is to be gained from this study?

There are four things I hope will be accomplished by a study on Hell. First, one of the most difficult things Christians struggle with is how the Doctrine of Hell can be reconciled with the nature of God. How can a loving God send people to Hell? What kind of a God would call His saints to rejoice in Heaven, if at the same time a greater part of human beings is suffering eternal punishments?

A great many believers have heard these critiques of the Doctrine of Hell but have never heard a biblical response. Some time ago, actor Stephen Fry, an atheist, was being interviewed regarding his rejection of God. He was being asked what he would say if he were confronted by God. He said, "Bone cancer in children? I would say to God, 'How dare you?'"

Some Christians, upon hearing this cheeky response in which an atheist imagines that he would be seated on a throne and call God to give an account, are left startled with no answer. Many of us have never heard a solid biblical answer regarding why it is God who sits on the throne of judgment, rather than we as human beings. So, we need to regain a deep sense of confidence in the truth of the gospel, in which God is righteous to judge human beings.

Second, we must put aside all the silly pictures we have of Hell. We must actually study the biblical passages that describe Hell to come to a clearer understanding of what it truly is. There are numerous false views that must be rejected. Instead, we must confess that Hell is eternal. Hell provides no opportunity for redemption. Hell does not end in annihilation; rather, Hell never ends.

Another false view is that God never sends anyone there, but rather we choose to go there against His objections. All of these views are ways to blunt the biblical material simply because of our embarrassment around the subject. A thorough biblical study on the actual nature of Hell will bring a great deal of sobriety into the discussion.

Third, we must examine the idea of Hell and Christian motivation for missions and evangelism.

Fourth, we need to reconnect the Doctrine of Hell to the Doctrine of Last Things. What is it that the Bible actually says about the last judgment? What is the basis upon which people are judged? Revelation 14:9–10 tells us that God is not absent from Hell, but is present to it in order to visit His enemies with His ceaseless wrath: "If anyone worships the beast and its image and receives a mark on his forehead or on his hand, he also will drink the wine of God's wrath, poured full strength into the cup of His anger, and he will be tormented with fire and sulfur in the presence of the holy angels and in the presence of the Lamb." These are terrifying words, and they indicate that a study of Hell is certainly called for.

I end this chapter with an invitation to think about that which we shudder to think about. We must do it with a great deal of reverence and foreboding. We must be reminded that our God is a consuming fire, and that He is not to be trifled with.

CHAPTER FOUR

HELL AND THE NATURE OF GOD

C. S. Lewis once said about Hell, "There is no doctrine which I would more willingly remove from Christianity than this, if it lay in my power."[8] In some ways we might all agree with him. Anyone with the mildest sense of compassion for other human beings is horrified by the idea of Hell. The question that often comes into our minds is, "What kind of a God would send someone there?" This chapter is dedicated to answering this question. If the Doctrine of Hell is deeply rooted in Scripture, just who is the God of the Bible?

God as holy, merciful, and majestic

Understanding the Doctrine of Hell begins with understanding who God is revealed to be in Scripture.

We begin in Exodus 33. The people of Israel have just sinned against God by making a golden calf idol (Exodus 32). Hardly had the Ten Commandments been given when they were already breaking the first and second. But the Israelites go further. In spite of the fact that they saw God's glorious rescue from Egypt,

---
[8] *The Problem of Pain*, C.S. Lewis. HarperOne, 2015.

they are now attempting to change history. They proclaim that these idols, not God, were responsible for bringing them out of Egypt. In response, God stands ready to consume them from the face of the earth. Moses pleads with God to have mercy. He tells the people of Israel he will go back up to Mount Sinai. He says, "Perhaps I can make atonement for your sin" (Exodus 32:30). At that point, Moses is not sure that God will accept his atonement and forgive him. Perhaps all that is left is the utter destruction of the people.

This background gives rise to the drama of Exodus 33. God begins by telling Moses He will indeed have mercy on the people: "Go up to a land flowing with milk and honey; but I will not go up among you, lest I consume you on the way, for you are a stiff-necked people. When the people heard this disastrous word, they mourned, and no one put on his ornaments" (Exodus 33:3–4).

And with that, Moses pitched a tent at a distance from the camp of Israel. This tent, called the "Tent of Meeting," came into being before the tabernacle was built. There, while many of the people watched, Moses would enter the tent and meet with God. Whenever Moses entered that tent, a pillar of cloud descended on it and the people would rise up looking at the sight of God among them meeting with Moses. And they would worship. For it was in that tent that Moses would cry out to God for mercy on behalf of a sinful people.

On one occasion, Moses seems to have left the tent and gone up onto Mount Sinai. It must have been a very special occasion. He is again praying for the people. And on this occasion, after much prayer, the answer finally comes: "And the LORD said to Moses, 'This very thing that you have spoken I will do, for you have found favor in my sight, and I know you by name'" (Exodus 33:17). This was a significant moment. After a lengthy season of intercession, God finally grants complete forgiveness and offers that much sought-after mercy.

In that profound and holy moment, Moses, overwhelmed with the graciousness and kindness of God, asks Him something he has never asked before: "Please show me your glory" (Exodus 33:18).

The majesty of God has overwhelmed Moses. Reveling in holy fear and delight, he asks one of the most audacious prayer requests in history: to see the glory and majesty of God. And God responds, "I will make all my goodness pass before you and will proclaim before you my name, the LORD. And I will be gracious to whom I will be gracious and will show mercy on whom I will show mercy. But you cannot see my face, for man shall not see me and live" (Exodus 33:19–20).

Standing before God is like standing before a nuclear blast and questioning it. No one can do that. Isaiah 33:14 says, "The sinners in Zion are afraid; trembling has seized the godless; 'Who among us can dwell with the consuming fire? Who among us can dwell with everlasting burnings?'" Psalm 119:119–120 tells us that "All the wicked of the earth you discard like dross, therefore I love your testimonies. My flesh trembles for fear of you, and I am afraid of your judgments."

Finally, regard Isaiah's description of the Day of the Lord: "And the haughtiness of man shall be humbled, and the lofty pride of men shall be brought low, and the LORD alone will be exalted in that day. And the idols shall utterly pass away. And people shall enter the caves of the rocks and the holes of the ground, from before the terror of the LORD, and from the splendor of his majesty, when he rises to terrify the earth" (Isaiah 2:17–19).

Remember Stephen Fry's words in the previous chapter? He says he would question God. In his mind, there is nothing there that should terrify him. He seems to indicate that his anger against God would put God on His heels. I suspect that is also what many others think as well. They have been used to thinking of Him as a capable human being, rather than God.

Fry seems to be saying, "Since you are more capable than the rest of us, why haven't you solved the disease questions?"

For many, the central and only attribute of God is supposed to be love, to the exclusion of all other attributes that Moses, the psalmist, and Isaiah saw. They saw God as holy, as just, mighty, and righteous. Of course God is love. But when we think of only one attribute of God at the expense of everything else, it becomes distorted and looks more like an idol of the mind than anything else.

God brings honour to His name

We need to recognize that God has many other attributes that make Him far more complex.

We can begin that process by reviewing one of the most well-known passages in the Bible. Psalm 23:1–3 begins with what many of us have memorized: "The LORD is my shepherd; I shall not want. He makes me lie down in green pastures. He leads me beside still waters. He restores my soul. He leads me in paths of righteousness." Many stop quoting verse three here, but the rest is important because it gives us the reason or the justification as to why God is so gracious towards us. The full verse reads, "He leads me in paths of righteousness *for his name's sake* [emphasis mine]."

When we end the verse too soon, we assume that the only important part is that the Lord is our Shepherd, and that He is watching over us, feeding us, restoring us, and leading us into righteousness for the sake of *our* own name. Or that He is blessing us because He is concerned for us. But Psalm 23 is adamant. God is doing these things not for our sake, but for His!

This is hard for some to comprehend. To say that God is blessing us for the sake of His name is to say that He does it for the sake of His pleasure, or for the sake of His reputation, or to be highly honoured. Immediately we imagine that God is only acting as He does for self-serving reasons.

Yet, fascinatingly enough, Psalm 23:3 is not the only place in the Bible where we hear God speaking this way. Psalm 25:11 contains a prayer of confession to God: "For your name's sake, O LORD, pardon my guilt." Psalm 31:3 says, "For you are my rock and my fortress; and for your name's sake you lead me and guide me." And Psalm 79:9 pleads, "Help us, O God of our salvation, for the glory of your name; deliver us, and atone for our sins, for your name's sake."

We are not restricted to the Psalms, either, to find such language. 1 Samuel 12:22 promises, "For the LORD will not forsake his people, for his great name's sake." Isaiah 37:35 also promises, "For I will defend this city to save it, for my own sake." And Isaiah 48:9 declares, "For my name's sake I defer my anger, for the sake of my praise I restrain it for you." Two verses later we read, "For my own sake, for my own sake, I do it, for how should my name be profaned? My glory I will not give to another" (Isaiah 48:11).

Imagine a politician who acts to provide some benefit for her constituency. And in a later interview, when asked what motivated her, she declares, "I did it for my own name's sake." Her leading motivation in whatever benevolent actions she performed was to enhance and advance her reputation. Almost all of us would find this to be scandalous. Whenever we find people whose ultimate purpose for their actions is to enhance their reputation, or to act for their own name's sake, we utterly condemn them. We think this to be narcissistic and unethical. And yet God says that is precisely what He does.

This brings us to the crux of the matter: why is it that God claims for Himself that which we condemn when we see it in everyone else? And God is not shy to say that He does all things for His glory. When we answer this conundrum, we come close to the beginning of all proper reasoning about God.

If our politician is acting for herself, we might respond by saying, "What about everyone else? Isn't their worth equal to your own?" Of course, we know there may be people in her constituency who are far less virtuous than she is, but there are no doubt some in her constituency who are far more virtuous than she. Still, virtue or not, most would say that her worth as a human being is the same as the worth of all human beings. To act as if her worth supersedes all others is to act unrighteously. For this reason, it is right to condemn the person whose motivations and actions are based on a belief that their worth is greater than others.

However, here lies the difference: if God acted as if His own worth was only the same as that of the sum total of the human race, He would be acting unrighteously. But the worth of the Creator, who not only created all that exists but who also sustains the universe at each moment, cannot be compared to all things that are dependent on Him. Furthermore, the attributes of God are perfect. His goodness, righteousness, wisdom, knowledge, power, and mercy are not only without equal, they are the very definition of the terms. We only know and understand virtue as it is reflected from His being. For all these reasons and more, the worth of God is infinitely above the worth of all other things. That is what it means for God to be God. When God evaluates His being as infinitely more valuable than all that He has made and all that He sustains, His evaluation of the worth of His being is not a subjective evaluation. God states this as objectively true. If God were to evaluate the sum total of all other things as being of equal value to Himself, He would be acting in an unethical manner. It would be shameful for God to act this way.

Imagine a human being choosing to save the life of a malaria-carrying insect rather than the life of an infant. Would we not utterly condemn that? Of course we would. We know that a child is worth so much more than an insect. But the worth of God is infinitely above the worth of the total of all that exists.

Therefore, it is righteous for God, at all points in time, to act with Himself as the key focus of all His concerns. And so, acting righteously, the Father is delighted in constantly expressing and affirming His delight in the worth of Himself.

The Benedictine monk, abbot, philosopher, and theologian Anselm of Canterbury (1033–1109) said, "God maintains nothing with more justice than the honour of his dignity."[9] The great American pastor and theologian Jonathan Edwards reminds us that God regards the glory of his name above all things.[10] And because of this, all of His creation should shout for joy. The God who exists is holy, righteous, merciful, good, and loving. And in response, the most righteous thing we can do is to learn to imitate God. Like Him, we too must do all things for His glory.

God will defend the glory of His name

Holding firmly to this biblical truth, let's press forward to the next logical conclusion. God's concern for His glory leads Him to a predictable action. We hear this in the second commandment: "You shall not make for yourself a carved image, or any likeness or anything that is in heaven above, or that is in the earth beneath, or that is in the water under the earth. You shall not bow down to them or serve them, for I the LORD your God am a jealous God, visiting the iniquity of the fathers on the children to the third and the fourth generation of those who hate me" (Exodus 20:4–5).

God identifies Himself as a jealous God. He declares that He is a God who will not be trifled with. If you or I prefer something to God, God declares He will act out of jealousy to defend the glory of His name. How unrighteous it would be for

---

[9] *Cur Deus Homo,* Anselm of Canterbury, 1094-1098
[10] *A Dissertation Concerning the End for Which God Created the World,* Jonathan Edwards, 1765.

God to do anything else. It would be like preferring a malaria-infested insect over a child. How wonderful that God is jealous for His glory.

Deuteronomy 28:15–19 shows us the extent of God's concern for His glory:

> But if you will not obey the voice of the LORD your God or be careful to do all his commandments and his statutes that I command you today, then all these curses shall come upon you and overtake you. Cursed shall you be in the city, and cursed shall you be in the field. Cursed shall be your basket and your kneading bowl. Cursed shall be the fruit of your womb and the fruit of your ground, the increase of your herds and the young of your flock. Cursed shall you be when you come in, and cursed shall you be when you go out.

The rest of the chapter details the curses. It warns of everything from diseases to drought to changes in weather to changes in the political climate to defeat before enemies on the battlefield. All of these are directed by the God who uses all His power, might, and energy to express delight in His glory. He declares that He will bless those who also revel in His glory and oppose fully those who dispute the worth of the one whose worth infinitely surpasses the combined weight of all other things.

Rather than remaining faithful to the covenant God made with them, Israel sinned and incurred the righteous wrath of God. Yet God would not break His covenant. Ezekiel 39:25 says, "Therefore thus says the Lord God: Now I will restore the fortunes of Jacob and have mercy on the whole house of Israel, and I will be jealous for my holy name."

Because God had made a covenant and placed His reputation on the line in keeping and maintaining it, He was now, in jealousy for His holy name, going to restore Israel. He would cause a national revival for holiness in the people and restore the nation. This renewal of God's people would result in the only good thing that could come of all that had transpired: God ensuring that His name was glorified.

The cross of Christ

The story of the cross of Christ parallels this tale of national revival. God would never forgive sinners if He were not jealous for His righteousness. But God is greatly glorified in the cross of His Son. The cross is a demonstration of how God feels about all assaults on His glory. The cross is God's declaration to the world: "That is what sin deserves." For there, at the cross, the Son becomes the sin-bearer for the world. There, seeing the sins of the world, the Father righteously poured out His wrath onto the Son. Nothing in all of history could so demonstrate how the Father deals with sin. For this reason, we can accurately conclude that the cross is the ultimate demonstration, both of the holiness of God and His sheer contempt for all that is unrighteous. It does not end there, though. Precisely because the Son went to the cross to display the glory of God, the cross also demonstrates the Father's esteem for His Son. As John 17:5 reminds us, on the cross the Son glorifies the Father. He does so in His perfect obedience to the Father, testifying that He is confident that His Father's plan in the cross is good and perfect. But the Father also glorifies the Son by demonstrating that on the cross the Son remains the object of the Father's delight.

Thus, it is not possible to speak about Heaven and Hell, or about the nature of God, without dealing with the meaning of the cross of Jesus. The cross speaks about mercy, wrath, justice, and the honour of obedience to the Father, all in the same breath.

The glory of God and the reality of Hell

Jesus is the image and glory of God. Revelation 19:15 describes to us what will happen when Jesus returns: "From his mouth comes a sharp sword with which to strike down the nations, and he will rule them with a rod of iron. He will tread the winepress of the fury of the wrath of God Almighty."

In the next chapter, Revelation 20:10, we learn of a lake of fire and sulfur in which souls are tormented day and night forever and ever. Verse 15 says, "If anyone's name was not found written in the book of life, he was thrown into the lake of fire." They were thrown into the lake to be tormented day and night for eternity.

In the realm of earthly affairs or human governments in which the rule of law and fairness pervades, we all agree that greater crimes merit greater punishments. No one would want to punish a person with a parking ticket in the same way we would punish those who have brought about the unjust death of another. Justice demands that the greater the crime, the greater the punishment. In the same vein, the lesser the infraction of law, the lesser the punishment. Indeed, if someone doesn't pay their parking fine, we don't rise up and demand justice. Not so with crimes against humanity.

No reasonable human being would disagree with this. The matter in which we profoundly disagree is when we assess how great a crime against God and His government over the creation He has made is. What do we make of the one who says that God is not God, that He is not all glorious, and that finding our delight in God is not just a religious choice, but the greatest moral imperative?

In his work entitled *The Eternity of Hell's Torments*, Jonathan Edwards argues that since the obligation to love, honour, and obey God is infinite, any violation of this obligation constitutes an infinite evil deserving of infinite punishment.

Edwards contends that the only way to evade this conclusion is by denying the infinite glory of God, who is sovereign ruler of the universe.[11]

Edwards is right and expresses the biblical view perfectly. A crime against humanity is a lesser crime than one against God. That's it! Failing to glorify that which demands worship is a crime so frighteningly evil that nothing but the full weight of God's wrath can be demanded.

For this reason, those who deny Hell of necessity also deny the infinite glory of God. This is the fundamental dividing line of all theologies. Wherever we find a person who does not believe that sin against God is an infinite crime demanding an infinite punishment, we also find a person who has constructed an idol in the place of the living God. Furthermore, God does not think that the worship of a substitute for Himself is a personal choice. He thinks it to be a monstrous evil.

I have, on occasion, been asked if people go to Hell for not believing in it. I usually want to roll my eyes. Hell is the consequence, not of failing to believe in Hell, but of failing to believe in the one true and living God. Those who hold the idea that failure to worship the true God is not an infinite evil are not thinking about the real God at all.

We should be overwhelmed by God's love

And that leads me to one final thought: we should be overwhelmed daily with the love of God. That a God who is perfectly satisfied in Himself, a God who does not need us, a God who desires to glorify His name should take delight in showing mercy to undeserving sinners should confound and overwhelm us. We should struggle to take it in. To think of the love of God as a given is to misunderstand that we are talking

---

[11] *The Eternity of Hell's Torments*, Jonathan Edwards, 1739.

about God. But once we understand the nature of God, love from Him is a staggering thought. That God should so love the world that he should give his only begotten Son, that whoever believes in him should not perish but have eternal life (John 3:16) is beyond our ability to grasp. Furthermore, that the one exalted Son who is the object of the Father's love should suffer the wrath of God in our place should leave us speechless. What then should be made of the person who rejects such an offer of grace?

And so the question is never "why is there suffering in this world?" nor "how could a God of love also be the God who would create Hell?" The greatest question is "how is it even conceivable that there should be good in the world, and that there would be such an outflow of mercy that would open the door to Heaven?"

In other words, the question is never "how can God allow Hell?" The question is always "how can God allow Heaven?"

CHAPTER FIVE

THE AWFUL NATURE OF HELL

The rich man and Lazarus

What happens to those who die whose sins are not atoned for? Here, Jesus helps us with a story:

> There was a rich man who was clothed in purple and fine linen and who feasted sumptuously every day. And at his gate was laid a poor man named Lazarus, covered with sores, who desired to be fed with what fell from the rich man's table. Moreover, even the dogs came and licked his sores. The poor man died and was carried by the angels to Abraham's side. The rich man also died and was buried, and in Hades, being in torment, he lifted up his eyes and saw Abraham far off and Lazarus at his side. [Luke 16:19–23]

This is clearly a terrifying scene, for several reasons. First, because the afterlife and its consequences happen immediately after death. Second, because the experience in Hell is spoken of in physical terms. When we discuss Heaven, I will say that it is not a spiritual experience alone; rather, it is a place with sights, sounds, smells, and tastes. It is tactile. We will experience Heaven as we experience life here. The same is true of Hell. However we understand our Lord's description of what occurred to the rich man, it should be clear that Jesus believed the unrighteous go immediately to Hades upon death and are instantly in a place of torment.

Here we are left to examine some of the parallels between Heaven and Hell. Clearly, just like Heaven, Hell ("Hades," in the above passage) happens immediately after death. There is no unconscious soul sleep or state of non-existence until the last day. Even though human beings are contingent beings, God has arranged matters so that when the body is torn from the spirit at death, the body dies but the spirit continues in conscious existence. This is shown when the rich man sees Lazarus, and as he expresses his own torment.

To say we are contingent beings is to say that our existence is not eternal. We do not continue to exist after death out of logical necessity. The soul is not an eternal entity. God alone is a non-contingent being. He is eternal. His existence is not dependent upon anything for its existence. He exists of logical necessity, but we do not. The only reason we survive our own death is because God, who wills all things, has willed that our soul will survive our death. Our soul is contingent on the willingness of God to continue to sustain us. Even as this is true in the present life, it continues to be true in the future.

It may be that those who die before the Second Coming of Christ are provided with a temporary physical existence before they receive their final body. Paul speaks of the soul being torn from the body at death as being "unclothed" (2 Corinthians 5:4). If God provides temporary clothing before the final receiving of a body that will not die, we would then anticipate a physical existence of the departed, even before the Second Coming. And this perspective, if it is correct, would explain Jesus's parable of the rich man and Lazarus. In some fashion, both the rich man and Lazarus have survived their own deaths. Both are experiencing their lives in a physical form. And this form of existence seems to predate the consummation of all things at the end of the age, because the brothers of the rich man are still alive on the earth.

From this vantage point, we are now in a place to continue to read the account. The rich man is physically suffering. His sense of thirst is overwhelming: "And he called out, 'Father Abraham, have mercy on me, and send Lazarus to dip the end of his finger in water and cool my tongue, for I am in anguish in this flame'" (Luke 16:24).

Let's assume that what Jesus is describing occurs in what we have called "the intermediate state." The current age continues on earth. However, the dead are now found in Abraham's side or in the place of torment, called Hades.

But time moves forward. Eventually, the living inhabitants of earth, and those who have died and are now either at Abraham's side or in Hades, finally arrive at the end of the current age. What then?

Jesus describes the end of the current age this way:

> When the Son of Man comes in his glory, and all the angels with him, then he will sit on his glorious throne. Before him will be gathered all the nations, and he will separate people one from another as a shepherd separates the sheep from the goats. And he will place the sheep on his right, but the goats on the left. Then the King will say to those on his right, "Come, you who are blessed by my Father, inherit the kingdom prepared for you from the foundation of the world. For I was hungry and you gave me food,

I was thirsty and you gave me drink, I was a stranger and you welcomed me, I was naked and you clothed me, I was sick and you visited me, I was in prison and you came to me." Then the righteous will answer him, saying, "Lord, when did we see you hungry and feed you, or thirsty and give you drink? And when did we see you a stranger and welcome you, or naked and clothe you? And when did we see you sick or in prison and visit you?" And the King will answer them, "Truly, I say to you, as you did it to one of the least of these my brothers, you did it to me."

Then he will say to those on his left, "Depart from me, you cursed, into the eternal fire prepared for the devil and his angels. For I was hungry and you gave me no food, I was thirsty and you gave me no drink, I was a stranger and you did not welcome me, naked and you did not clothe me, sick and in prison and you did not visit me." Then they also will answer, saying, "Lord, when did we see you hungry or thirsty or a stranger or naked or sick or in prison, and did not minister to you?" Then he will answer them, saying, "Truly, I say to you, as you did not do it to one of the least of these, you did not do it to me." And these will go away into eternal punishment, but the righteous into eternal life." [Matthew 25:31–46]

There are so many things that capture the imagination in this section, and so many things about which we might wish to ask questions. What was Jesus talking about when He spoke of seeing him "naked and hungry and in prison?" Who exactly was Jesus speaking about when He spoke of the "least of these my brothers"? That in itself is a fascinating study that deserves our attention.

But for our purposes, I don't want to lose sight of the theme of this chapter. How is Hell described? And what are the events that lead to that final destination?

Eternity of Heaven and Hell

In Matthew 25, Jesus is describing His role on the final great Day of Judgment. He says that every human being who has ever lived will one day stand before Him. This will include those whose sins are atoned for and those whose sins remain unforgiven. Like a shepherd, He passes through the mass of the human race and puts everyone into one of two groups.

Notice the pairing of the words in verse 46: eternal punishment and eternal life. If, as some argue, Hell is not of endless duration, then by the very nature of the language found in this text, neither is Heaven. But clearly Jesus's choice of words indicates that both the life that the righteous will receive and the punishment that the unrighteous receive are eternal. *Eternal* means what it indicates—it is unending. There is no evading the force of this argument. If Hell is of a limited duration, then so is Heaven. But, as is clearly the case in Jesus's teaching, because Heaven is of an unlimited duration, so also is Hell. Both are eternal.

There is one more important scripture passage to consider that offers us a glimpse of what Hell is like:

> Then I saw a great white throne and him who was seated on it. From his presence earth and sky fled away, and no place was found for them. And I saw the dead, great and small, standing before the throne, and books were opened. Then

another book was opened, which is the book of life. And the dead were judged by what was written in the books, according to what they had done. And the sea gave up the dead who were in it, Death and Hades gave up the dead who were in them, and they were judged, each one of them, according to what they had done. Then Death and Hades were thrown into the lake of fire. This is the second death, the lake of fire. And if anyone's name was not found written in the book of life, he was thrown into the lake of fire. [Revelation 20:11–15]

Notice that the lake of fire is also referred to as the "second death." And this is the answer to those who say that the Bible only *threatens* that the unrighteous will die. But as we have already seen, all that occurs at the point of death is the tearing of the soul from the body. The physical body dies, but the soul or the spirit continues to live. This is the first death. Following that, at the end of the present age there exists a second death. It is as if the suffering souls of Hades are put to death a second time. On this occasion they are thrown into the lake of fire, and it is this that is intended when the Bible finally reveals all that is meant by the term *death*.

Putting it all together

It should now be plain that the Bible teaches that the souls of those who die without having their sins forgiven are taken immediately to a place of torment. And then, before the final judgment, all the unrighteous dead receive their resurrection bodies. Then, physically standing before the throne, they are judged according to what they have done. Every human being will be found to have fallen short of the glory of God. Every sin will be recounted. This must include all the actions that have been done. Also included will be all the thoughts they have had, as well as their private and secret actions. At the heart of all judgment will be the examination of each moment. Was this life lived for the glory of God or not? Nothing will be left unexamined.

What is Hell like?

From Jesus's parable in Matthew and John's vision in Revelation we gain a horrifying picture. First, it is a prison. Second, it is a pit, also called the "bottomless pit." Third, it is a place of everlasting burning. Fourth, it is a place of darkness. Finally, it is a place where God's anger is forever and ceaselessly poured out.

Let's review these images one at a time. First, we have the image of a prison. Since we know that Hell is described as the place God has reserved for the devil and his angels, we can therefore assume that the same eternal place of the demons is also the place of the damned: "For if God did not spare angels when they sinned, but cast them into Hell and committed them to chains of gloomy darkness to be kept until the judgment . . . The Lord knows how to rescue the godly from trials, and to keep the unrighteous under punishment until the day of judgment" (2 Peter 2:4,9).

At the very least, Hell is compared to a prison house that includes chains and is intensely dark and gloomy. Should we think of this as a literal description? Or is Peter using images that his readers can relate to? While I can't answer definitively, I think we do well to imagine a literal description. This is because we are encouraged to think of Hell as a material place. Like Heaven, it is not simply a spiritual reality. It is an altogether horrifying picture.

Second, Hell is compared to a bottomless pit. Some translations simply call this the "abyss." Isaiah 14, in a passage that records a taunt against the king of Babylon, who must have seemed so powerful to Israel, shows his final destiny. Verse 11 says, "Your pomp is brought down to Sheol." The image is that the king of Babylon has suffered the loss of everything he has ever had. But in so doing he has not gone up. He has gone down, farther than he could have imagined: "But you are brought down to Sheol, to the far reaches of the pit" (Isaiah 14:15). The image is of a vast underground chamber.

How deep is this pit? According to Revelation 9, the pit has no bottom. It continues to go down forever. The idea that captures our minds is that the abyss is a place of vastness that contains infinite room. It is impossible to plumb its depths. One can imagine not just the size but also the darkness.

Third, Hell is a place of everlasting burning. This is one of the most common images of Hell. Listen to Jesus's description of it: "Just as the weeds are gathered and burned with fire, so will it be at the end of the age. The Son of Man will send his angels, and they will gather out of his kingdom all causes of sin and all law-breakers, and throw them into the fiery furnace. In that place there will be weeping and gnashing of teeth" (Matthew 13: 40–42).

Or consider the words of Revelation 14:10. Speaking of the ungodly, it says, "He also will drink the wine of God's wrath, poured full strength into the cup of his anger, and he will be tormented with fire and sulfur in the presence of the holy angels and in the presence of the Lamb."

Notice that God is present in Hell. This should not surprise us, for He is omnipresent. In His righteousness, He is there to ensure that the just punishment to the crimes against His holiness is carried out to exacting detail. The citizens of Hell are unable to escape Him. We recall the words in Psalm 139:7–8: "Where shall I go from your Spirit? Or where shall I flee from your presence? If I ascend to heaven, you are there! If I make my bed in Sheol, you are there!"

Consider the finality of Revelation 14:11: "And the smoke of their torment goes up forever and ever, and they have no rest, day or night."

I am overwhelmed with terror as I think of these things. And to be truthful, the reason the Scripture pulls back the curtain and exposes these things is so that we might consider the gravity of the moment in which we find ourselves. Life is not without its consequences, nor are our actions devoid of meaning. Furthermore, the servants of Christ must see what comes when we are complacent in the sharing of the gospel.

Hell is not only a prison, it is a great and endless pit, a massive cavern of darkness that has no bottom. Third, Hell is a place of endless burning and torment. Fourth, Hell is a place of darkness. And if the fire is to be thought of as literal, one would have to imagine that it is a dark fire.

Notice how often the Bible contrasts the themes of light and darkness. John 3:19–20 says that the condemnation of the wicked is that they preferred darkness over light. Psalm 82 says the wicked walk in darkness. And 1 Thessalonians 5:5 says that those who continue to sin are the children of darkness. Therefore, Jude 13 speaks of the gloom of utter darkness that has been reserved forever.

However, based on a reading of 2 Thessalonians 1:9, some think that Hell is a place where its occupants are safe from God after all: "They will suffer the punishment of eternal destruction, away from the presence of the Lord and from the glory of his might." That is, they suffer away from the glory of the might of God. But to understand 2 Thessalonians 1:9 rightly, we do well to read the next verse: "When he comes on that day to be glorified in his saints, and to be marveled at among all who have believed" (Verse 10). The passage is not saying that the inhabitants of Hell are safe from God. Rather, on the day of the saints' greatest joy, when our Lord reveals Himself in glory to His elect and we shall see Him as He is, with eyes flowing with tears of joy, hands raised, multitudes shouting with joy, the greatest moment in human history, those in Hell are excluded because of the dungeon to which they have been consigned.

And so, according to Jesus and the rest of our Bible, Hell is the place where the unrighteous are forever punished. They live bodily and never escape the torment that is reserved for them. This occurs because God is righteous.

There may still be unanswered and troubling questions that remain from the Bible's description of Hell. The first is "why would anyone believe in Hell?" I have sometimes been asked why I do. My first response is always that I believe in Hell because my Lord and Saviour Jesus Christ believed in it, and He taught on the matter frequently. But I also believe in it because the very nature of God and His supremacy over all things is the very definition of good and evil. It is an infinite evil to turn one's back against God. Furthermore, I also note that my salvation means so much more to me when I discover what it is I have been redeemed from. And so I find that the idea of Hell, as horrible as the matter is, demands I face it and come to terms with its awful nature.

What should we do now?

What shall we say of this troubling picture of Hell? We should say, "Oh God, until now I had no idea how holy You are. Until now I had no idea how serious my sin is." We should also say, "I had only a small notion of how great an offer is made to me in Christ."

According to the scene of the final judgment in Revelation, the only hope any of us have is not that, when our actions are examined, we will be found to have passed the test. God does not hold a pair of scales in His hand, weighing our evil deeds against our righteous ones. Clearly, this is not the image. Rather, according to the Book of Revelation, the only hope any of us have is that our names have been recorded in the Book of Life. If so, we are saved the eternal punishment awaiting the world. If our name is absent, every action of our lives has been judged and recorded in the book. Not one action of our life was overlooked. There is no withstanding such scrutiny. Everyone will have been found to have fallen short of the Creator's righteous expectations.

To put the matter plainly, either our lives are hidden in Christ, or they are not. Either Christ has paid for our sins because of His death on the cross, or the righteous punishment for our sins remains unpaid. Either we are judged based on Christ's righteous life, or on our unrighteous one. Either Christ has been substituted for us, or we stand before the throne based on our track record.

Therefore, it is urgent to consider these matters. If you have not done so, confess to Christ that God has already judged you and found that you fell short—that you are a sinner. Confess that Jesus is the Son of God. Trust that He lived and died so that you might have your name written in the Book of Life. Actively surrender and submit your life and future into His hands. Ask Him to save you from the just punishment to come. For unless Christ is your life, your judgment will be based on how you lived your life.

CHAPTER SIX

A FEW REMAINING QUESTIONS

Imagine a young man wooing a young woman. She is not sure about him, and eventually she decides she is not interested. Because the young man is a gentleman, he allows the young woman to go her own way. Of course, she is free to choose her own pathway in life.

Some imagine this is an accurate picture of God and His dealings with the human race. He is wooing us, telling us that we are His creation and that we were made for Him. But so many resist. However, because God is a gentleman, He allows us to go our own way. He is sad about it, but He respects the integrity of our choices. Many contemporary Christians are accustomed to thinking about Hell in this way.

Isn't Hell just a choice to deny a relationship with God?

In this scenario, Hell is not a place of torment. Rather, it is merely the place where we never enter the joy of knowing our Creator. It is God saying, *If you want to live without me, I will let you do that. I am a gentleman. It is not about justice, but only about a relationship that will never happen.*

For many, this absence of relationship with God is the only conception of Hell they have been taught. So, when they begin to read the scripture, especially the teachings of Jesus, they are shocked, as they soon see that this typical modern-day picture of Hell is simply not found in the Bible.

There is an emotional response to the biblical picture of Hell. Many reject it because it seems too horrifying to contemplate. Many argue that if one believes in Hell, one must also believe in a God who is a torturer. How can God be filled with joy when at every moment in eternity there are poor damned souls in Hell? Can it be that God is delighted in Himself when He knows of His own creatures whose suffering never ends and whose misery continues at the present moment? Is this matter even vaguely conceivable?

Degrees of punishment

Regarding degrees of suffering in Hell, three things demand our attention. First, we see from reading the biblical material that there seems to be degrees of punishment in Hell. Furthermore, if it is true that not everyone in Hell suffers with the same intensity, we must also assume that the punishment given to each person is designed uniquely for them. This tells us that Hell is not a blunt instrument of torture, but rather the expression of God's perfect and infinite justice.

Jesus talked about degrees of punishment. In Luke 12:47–48, He says, "And that servant who knew his master's will but did not get ready or act according to his will, will receive a severe beating. But the one who did not know, and did what deserved a beating, will receive a light beating. Everyone to whom much was given, of him much will be required, and from him to whom they entrusted much, they will demand the more."

Jesus is warning the people who lived in the cities where He did his miracles that the greater the crime is against His

Kingdom, the greater will be the punishment. Indeed, Jesus warns exactly this to the people of Capernaum, who were present and witnessed the great majority of Jesus's miracles: "And you, Capernaum, will you be exalted to heaven? You will be brought down to Hades. For if the mighty works done in you had been done in Sodom, it would have remained until this day. But I tell you, that it will be more tolerable on the day of judgment for the land of Sodom than for you" (Matthew 11:23-24).

Notice the phrase "more tolerable." Are we to believe that Hell will be more tolerable for some than for others? Evidently so! That is exactly what Jesus taught. Furthermore, Jesus was frequently heard to remark, "Great will be your reward in Heaven." Jesus taught varying degrees of reward in Heaven, and He also taught of degrees of punishment in Hell.

When we reconsider the emotional response to Hell, we must ask if we are in a position to accuse God of being a torturer. In order to answer, we might do well in describing an actual torturer. Perhaps images of the Middle Ages come to mind, in which an inquisitor has his hapless victim strapped to a rack. Hot tongs were sometimes used to tear out chunks of flesh, accompanied by the horrid cries of the victim. Is this an adequate picture of Hell? No, it is not. Although medieval depictions of Hell were portrayed in this fashion, the biblical picture should not be confused with this horribly distorted view.

First, notice that the picture of the torturer is that of attempting to get the victim to confess to something before he is put to death. Torture is exerted to extract information. Perhaps the person being tortured is supposed to give away his associates, or to renounce his religious beliefs, or perhaps it is merely a matter of a vendetta. But in every case, the torture is happening without a trial.

None of that is true about Hell. According to the Bible, Hell follows the most precise, objective, and righteous trial in human history. According to Revelation 20:12, "And the dead were judged by what was written in the books, according to what they had done." To put that into terms we can easily grasp, consider the biblical picture. After the final resurrection, each human being appears before God. Like in a trial in which every single action, thought, intent, and failure to act is considered, each millisecond of an entire life lived will also be examined with the utmost detail. When God pronounces His sentence, it will include the exact conditions of Hell that strictly corresponds to the crimes done against His kingdom and His great name. Hell is not the crude club of a torturer. Rather, it is the exacting justice of the One who does all things well.

But still, someone might argue that they are not satisfied with this explanation of things. If, as the Bible describes it, sin is an infinite evil against an infinitely good and righteous God, deserving of an infinite punishment, we are still left with an overwhelmingly abhorrent picture of Hell. And it is this picture, not the justification of it, that troubles many of us.

But while this is a strong emotional reaction to such a doctrine, we need to ask, "What is the alternative?"

Our problem with God

The problem that so many of us have with Hell is actually our problem with God. If we are truthful, many of us can't conceive of a God who is infinitely worthy of all praise, adoration, and worship. We struggle with the idea that worship is the ultimate moral mandate. While we might mouth these words, we may confess that we actually hate them. For if we are honest about our feelings on this matter, we assume it is us as human beings who are ultimately worthy of all praise. Our happiness is the highest good for many, rather than the praises of Him who is of inestimable worth.

In truth, the scandal of the Doctrine of Hell has exposed the reality that many in our day are less offended by the idea of

Hell than they are by the doctrine of God. That God would be glorified in expressing His justice on the unrighteous is more than some of us can bear. After all, we reason in our hearts, who does God think He is? And to that, God responds that He thinks He is God!

So, we have come full circle. We began this chapter by recounting the popular way of describing Hell: it is a place human beings choose to go, not where God righteously metes out judgment. We imagine a God who is encouraging us not to go, but we refuse His counsel and decide that a life without God is better.

Given that this picture is entirely incongruous with the Bible, let's add another problem with this picture.

Too many of us believe that we are in control of our relationship with God. We are confident we can choose for Him or against Him as an act of our own will. We reason that we are in control of our own future, and bristle at the suggestion that we are not. Therefore, we imagine that Heaven and Hell are subject to our will and not to God's. In essence, we are the gods and He our servant, giving us what we demand. God, we think, is in our hands, and not we in His. God is then seen not as the prime mover but the eternal responder, limited in His actions by our first move. That is the image of the woman making a decision as to whether she wants to respond to her potential lover, which I presented at the beginning of the chapter.

But the words of the scripture never speak as our imaginations do. Ephesians 2:1–3 says, "And you were dead in the trespasses and sins in which you once walked, following the course of this world, following the prince of the power of the air, the spirit who is now at work in the sons of disobedience—among whom we all once lived in the passions of our flesh, carrying out the desires of the body and the mind, and were by nature children of wrath, like the rest of mankind."

Note Paul's choice of words: "dead in trespasses and sins." I know this about dead men and women: they don't rise from the dead by an act of their own will. They are not in charge of their relationship with life or death, never mind being in charge of their destiny. They are dead. You can plead with dead men to rise, but they will be unresponsive. Paul made that clear in Romans 3:11, where he said, "No one seeks God."

In Ephesians 2, after having described our condition before our conversion, Paul then describes our conversion. Instead of allowing us to say that we had the sense to see the matter clearly, Paul interrupts. He will not allow us to take any credit for salvation. Instead, when we read verses 4–5, Paul says, "But God, being rich in mercy, because of his great love with which he loved us . . . made us alive together with Christ." Our conversion, says Paul, is a resurrection from the dead brought about by the only One who can raise the dead.

And so, if you have in the past or are presently hearing the voice of Christ calling you to repent of your sins, it is up to you to respond. But lest you think you now control this relationship, think again. Who gave your dead ears the ability to hear the voice of God?

For while you thought you controlled your relationship with God, you were by nature a child of wrath. But when God opened your eyes, you saw that He is righteous, and you are not. You saw that He rules all things, and that you rule nothing. The great wonder of the Doctrine of Hell is that God, being rich in mercy, has sent His Son to spare you from that which you rightfully deserve.

Warning others of Hell

This leads us then to the last of our unanswered questions. Is it ever appropriate to call on people to repent by warning them of Hell? Should we also warn people about falling into sin lest they go to Hell? Should we feel a greater urgency to bring the gospel to the world because of the reality of the great cataclysm that awaits the human race? Is the Doctrine of Hell to be used in motivation, or are we only to use love as a motivation?

Thankfully, the answers to these questions are not in doubt. We need look no further than Jesus and imitate what He did. Let's concentrate on several passages from the book of Matthew:

> But I say to you that everyone who is angry with his brother will be liable to judgment; whoever insults his brother will be liable to the council; and whoever says, "You fool!" will be liable to the hell of fire. [Matthew 5:22]

> If your right eye causes you to sin, tear it out and throw it away. For it is better that you lose one of your members than that your whole body be thrown into hell. [Matthew 5:29]

> Enter by the narrow gate. For the gate is wide and the way is easy that leads to destruction, and those who find it are many. [Matthew 7:13]

> And do not fear those who kill the body but cannot kill the soul. Rather fear him who can destroy both soul and body in hell. [Matthew 10:28]

> And you, Capernaum, will you be exalted to heaven? You will be brought down to Hades [or to the place of torment. [Matthew 11:23]

> I tell you, on the day of judgment people will give account for every careless word they speak,

for by your words you will be justified, and by your words you will be condemned. [Matthew 12:36–37]

As part of the parable of the wheat and the tares:

> Let both grow together until the harvest, and at harvest time I will tell the reapers, "Gather the weeds first and bind them in bundles to be burned." [Matthew 13:30]

A part of the parable of the wedding feast:

> Bind him hand and foot and cast him into the outer darkness. In that place there will be weeping and gnashing of teeth. [Matthew 22:13]

> You serpents, you brood of vipers, how are you to escape being sentenced to hell? [Matthew 23:33]

A part of the parable of the wicked servant:

> The master of that servant will come on a day when he does not expect him and at an hour he does not know and will cut him in pieces and put him with the hypocrites. In that place there will be weeping and gnashing of teeth. [Matthew 24:50–51]

> And cast the worthless servant into the outer darkness. In that place there will be weeping and gnashing of teeth. [Matthew 25:30]

> And these will go into eternal punishment, but
> the righteous into eternal life. [Matthew 25:46]

I don't know how to make the matter plainer than simply to show that no one motivated people more by threatening hellfire on them than Jesus. He believed that if we keep on sinning and do not stop and repent, we will go to Hell. He believed that if we act hypocritically, we will go to Hell. He believed that if you slander another human being, you will go to Hell. He believed that you might not be punished for your wickedness in this life, but the time of judgment is coming. At that time, the majority of the human race will be thrown into Hell.

On this note, one must wonder: is the prevalence of gross and scandalous sins that many Christian leaders have fallen to due to the possibility that these people do not fear Hell? Is the prevalence of jokes about Hell among Christians an indication that we do not believe it to be a great danger? Is the demand for holiness among God's people frequently ignored because Hell is the last thing on our minds? Is our lack of teaching on Hell part of the reason why a renewal of holiness is not considered the greatest moral imperative we face? Failure to speak of Hell comes with consequences.

Furthermore, Jesus said that people in Hell would be gnashing their teeth. That's not an image of pain. It is an image of anger. All manner of people will have deluded themselves into believing that they are going to Heaven. That is their expectation. It is what they have been taught all their lives. They are convinced of their own inherent goodness, and they believe they have lived in such a way as to deserve to be in Heaven. But then they find themselves in Hell. In disbelief and horror, they grind their teeth in unbridled rage. They want to say to God, "How dare you?"

It is for this reason that the subject of Hell needs to be revived in our consideration. We must use this awful subject matter as motivation, just like Jesus did. We are in danger of deceiving people that their rightful place is Heaven.

Finally, we must also learn more about Hell so that we might more fully love our Saviour. For those of us who have been redeemed, we need to constantly remind ourselves that Jesus was tormented on our behalf. He who deserved only Heaven willingly chose to suffer under the wrath of the Father on my behalf. What wondrous love is this?

CHAPTER SEVEN

WHAT HAPPENS WHEN A BELIEVER DIES?

For those who trust in Christ alone for salvation and are facing your own death, this chapter will be of great encouragement. And for those of you who have had a loved one who has recently died in the Lord, this chapter will make the grieving process rich. For you are not to grieve as those who have no hope. In 1 Corinthians 15:55, the Apostle Paul writes, "O death, where is your victory, O death, where is your sting." Properly understood, the study of what happens to a believer at death should take away its sting.

Why do Christians suffer and die?

Before we get to the question of what occurs at death, let's answer a prior question. Why do Christians get sick, suffer, and die? We know that both believers and unbelievers die, but for believers, death is not punishment and cannot be related to our sins. Romans 8:1 teaches that there is no condemnation for those who are in Christ Jesus. Christ has removed our condemnation by being condemned on our behalf. He suffered and died in our place.

So why do we suffer? One answer is given to us in Hebrews 12:6: "For the Lord disciplines the one he loves, and chastises every son whom he receives." Later on in the same chapter we are told that we are to endure all hardship as discipline, as discipleship, or as training. God is treating us as sons. Hardship, suffering, and death trains us not to set our hopes in this earth, but in God.

Therefore, Christians should view the aging process, accompanied by sickness and eventually death, as God's plan to discipline us so that we might grow in sanctification, relying more and more on His power rather than our own. We learn not to put our hopes in this world, but to trust in the unseen hand of He who has made eternal promises to us.

Are there other reasons believers in Christ suffer and die? Yes, there are. In Philippians 3:10, Paul writes, "That I may know him and the power of his resurrection, and may share his sufferings, becoming like him in his death." God does not bring about the death of believers because of the fall or our own sins. Furthermore, it is not randomness that rules the world. Disease in our lives, along with accompanying weakness and the eventual dissolution of this body, is not the luck of the draw, or our bad genes. Rather, according to Paul, God allows us to be made holy through suffering. Furthermore, He is concerned that we might share a union with Christ. We taste death so that we might know what our Saviour tasted for us in order that we might identify with Him and love Him who died for us.

Look at it this way. When my oldest daughter first moved out of our house, she came home one day and announced, "Do you know how expensive groceries are?" I smiled and said, "No, honey, I don't. Are they expensive?" My daughter smiled and rolled her eyes. That was how her father often acted, but I had a method in my comments. I wanted her to understand that when she grew up in our house, our costly act of love was to pay the grocery bills for her. Now, for the first time, by paying those bills herself she had realized the expense of what we had done. We didn't want her to feel guilty, but we did want her to understand the extent of our love for her.

That is what death does for believers. In mercy, God allows His children to taste death so that we might see His great love in sending His son to die for us. When we arrive on Heaven's shore, we will say, "I never knew how great the sacrifice was that you paid for me. But when I tasted death, in a small and yet significant way, I identified with yours. So that is what it was for you, Jesus, to choose death! It was such a costly choice."

That is what God intended in our death. For endless ages, the words "Christ died for us" will be so much more significant. We will feel all the more loved.

How should believers think about death?

But how should believers think about death, either their own or those close to them? Let's again read the words of the apostle Paul: "For me to live is Christ, and to die is gain. If I am to live in the flesh, that means fruitful labor for me. Yet which I shall choose I cannot tell. I am hard pressed between the two. My desire is to depart and be with Christ, for that is far better" (Philippians 1:21–23). As the apostle Paul was facing the possibility of his own death, he felt the pull of two competing desires. On the one hand, he wished to stay alive for the ministry that Christ had assigned to him. It was overwhelmingly fruitful. But on the other hand, the idea of dying did not fill him with fear or uncertainty. He had already deeply embraced the idea that to die is better by far.

That same sentiment is expressed in Revelation 14:13: "And I heard a voice from heaven saying, 'Write this: Blessed are the dead who died in the Lord from now on.'" The Bible pronounces that, for all believers, death is not a curse but a blessing. And it is to this blessing that we now turn.

What happens when a believer dies?

When anyone dies their body expires, but not their soul. For the first time in their lives they experience the tearing apart of body and soul. It is at this point that many wonder what will happen. Can the soul exist apart from the body? Until this moment, the soul has thought, felt, experienced, grown, and learned through the body. The soul functions within and through the body in the physical world. Can that activity continue without the body? And if so, how? Furthermore, God designed our bodies to work in harmony with our souls. When He did so, He said it was good. Indeed, the book of Genesis portrays God as creating Adam from the dust of the earth and then breathing His breath into him. We can then say that it is the immaterial soul that gives life to the body. Throughout our lifetime, this is the only reality we have known. The human experience is one of an earthly and a spiritual dimension at the same time. God pronounces this experience as very good.

Again, we are left to wonder what happens when the soul is torn from the body. The answer is involved. Before we attempt a reasonable answer, let's consider the matter of "soul sleep." According to some, the soul falls asleep at death and falls into unconscious existence, awaiting to be awakened at the last resurrection. This view of things is often justified by the fact that the Bible sometimes uses the words "to fall asleep" as a metaphor for death. For instance, Acts 7:60 uses those words when Stephen, the first martyr, died. There it says, "He fell asleep."

But sleep is never a metaphor for unconscious existence. As we know, we dream when we sleep, and our brain is active and refreshes itself. Therefore, sleep is an appropriate metaphor for death, because just like when we fall asleep, we will awaken. And it is to this awakening that the Bible speaks.

The dead in Christ

But how and when? Paul's words in 1 Thessalonians 4:13-18 are instructive:

> But we do not want you to be uninformed, brothers, about those who are asleep, that you may not grieve as others do who have no hope. For since we believe that Jesus died and rose again, even so, through Jesus, God will bring with him those who have fallen asleep. For this we declare to you by a word from the Lord, that we who are alive, who are left until the coming of the Lord, will not precede those who have fallen asleep. For the Lord himself will descend from heaven with a cry of command, with the voice of an archangel, and with the sound of the trumpet of God. And the dead in Christ will rise first. Then we who are alive, who are left, will be caught up together with them in the clouds to meet the Lord in the air, and so we will always be with the Lord. Therefore encourage one another with these words.

When Christ returns at the end of this current age, all those who have died in Him will follow as He comes to rightfully reclaim this earth as His own. Paul is wanting to give hope to believers who wonder what has become of those among them who have died. Will they not participate in the Second Coming of Christ? But Paul reassures them that the believing dead will indeed have a wonderful part to play in the coming of Christ.

The dead in Christ will rise first, he says. That is, they will rise just prior to His coming and join Him in His glorious triumph. Clearly, the 1 Thessalonians account is collapsed. What is referred to in 1 Thessalonians is also discussed in Revelation 20:1-6. There we get an expanded picture of not just the dead in Christ, but the martyrs who have died in Him. They will be given a special place of honour: "They came to life and reigned with Christ for a thousand years" (Verse 4). And then it said the rest of the dead—that is, the unrighteous dead, those whose sins were not forgiven—did not come to life until the thousand years are ended.

Revelation 20:6 calls this the first resurrection: "Blessed and holy is the one who shares in the first resurrection!" This means that there is a second resurrection. Interestingly, Revelation doesn't refer to it as the "second resurrection." Instead, it calls this resurrection the "second death." One thousand years after the first resurrection comes the second death. The thought expressed is straightforward: blessed are those who are a part of the first resurrection, for they will have no part in the second death. As we have seen, the second death is the resurrection of the damned.

Coming back to our 1 Thessalonians text, Paul tells the believers that they should know this, so they will not grieve as those who have no hope. Those of us who are left alive when Christ returns, he says, will not receive our resurrection ahead of those who have died. That would indicate that the dead in Christ, just like we who are alive, are right now awaiting the resurrection. They are also awaiting the Second Coming.

Some have argued that these two passages seem to indicate that the dead in Christ are asleep, or that in some ways they are not conscious until the coming of Christ. Why else do they need a resurrection? If that were so, we might argue that they "rest in peace" until the Second Coming of Jesus. That is, they are not conscious now, or aware of anything until God makes them new at the first resurrection. At that moment they are again made body and soul.

But this view is surely wrong. If we examine everything the Bible says about the death of believers, we must also consider 2 Corinthians 5:6–9: "So we are always of good courage. We know that while we are at home in the body we are away from the Lord, for we walk by faith, not by sight. Yes, we are of good courage, and we would rather be away from the body and at home with the Lord. So, whether we are at home or away, we make it our aim to please him."

Notice Paul's wording—to be away from the body refers to death. At the moment of death, the believer is at home with the Lord. And just like in Philippians, Paul says if he had a choice his desire is to depart (or die), and at that time to be with Christ. This same perspective is in 2 Corinthians, where Paul affirms that he would rather be away from the body. I would rather die, he says, for the minute I do, I am with the Lord. And in Philippians 1:23 this state, in which the believer has died, is "far better." This must mean that the estate of the believing dead is far superior and much more desirable than what they experienced while they were alive in the body on earth.

It is hard to imagine how unconscious soul sleep is "better by far." Indeed, it is not. Even though the dead are anxiously awaiting the first resurrection, or the resurrection of the body, Paul affirms that they are in the presence of Christ, and their situation is infinitely better than the one they enjoyed while living on earth. That is why Paul says in Philippians that it was a sacrifice for him to stay alive.

Since the doctrine of soul sleep is not scriptural, and since the death of a believer is a blessed event that introduces the believer to a life that is better by far, how are we to understand the experience of the dead in Christ? Bible teachers, myself included, prefer to use the words "intermediate state" to describe the experience of a believer who has died now. We say it is an "intermediate state" because, as we have seen, it is not the final state of the believer.

It has become common to say that when a believer dies, they are now "in Heaven." Yes, they are. But what do we actually mean by that? Imagine that the pathway to our final eternal dwelling comes in a number of stages. Of course, we are born into sin, and we have inherited a sin nature resulting from Adam's fall. Then when we come to Christ something wonderful happens. According to John 5:24, Jesus says, "Truly, truly, I say to you, whoever hears my word and believes him who sent me has eternal life. He does not come into judgment, but has passed from death to life." That would mean that at the very moment anyone comes to confess their sins and entrust their lives into Christ's loving hands, they have at that moment already crossed over from death to life. The eternal life of God has already taken root in our hearts. This is true of all of us who know Christ as Saviour and Lord. Conversion is the first stage of the life to come. It is called the "new birth." We already know that we have received a foreshadowing of eternity now. Heaven has already touched us. We have a foretaste. Then comes the next stage. Jesus speaks of this in John 5:25: "Truly, truly, I say to you, an hour is coming, and is now here, when the dead will hear the voice of the Son of God, and those who hear will live." Jesus is stating that the dead who die in the Lord now hear the voice of the Son of God and live. That is, whenever a believer dies, he or she immediately hears Christ calling him or her, and they live in His presence.

However, as we have seen, while this is better by far from the life we experience on earth, it is still not the last stage, or the final reward that God has prepared for us.

In His presence

I have borrowed an illustration from author Randy Alcorn, changed it, and adopted it as my own. Imagine you lived in Tuktoyaktuk, which is on the northern end of the Northwest

Territories, far above the Arctic Circle. Imagine you are living there in winter when the sun never rises. But you have a good house with a great deal of amenities. Life is good. Then imagine you are told that a rich and gracious benefactor has purchased a property for you just outside of Honolulu. It is a wonderful house in a warm climate that has oceanfront property. You are told of water that is not frozen and of going outside with shorts and a short-sleeved shirt and sandals. You rejoice at the thought. You can only imagine a land where you never have to fight the twenty-four-hour darkness again.

You might object to my illustration. Surely our present life is better than Tuktoyaktuk in the middle of the winter. But remember also that this life is one where sin, death, rebellion, and evil live. Even though we have received eternal life from the Spirit as a down-payment, we constantly live in the valley of the shadow of death.

Now imagine the day of your move has arrived. You have a plane ticket and you will be transported to your new destination. But then you are told there will be one stopover. You will land in the city of Vancouver before your connecting flight takes you to your final destination. Given its location, Vancouver is exceedingly warm in January. As you arrive, you look out of the plane's windows and notice there is no snow. It is raining. Furthermore, you will be there several days. You get out and notice that even though it rains a lot, the sun rises every day. This is better than Tuktoyaktuk by far. But this is not your final destination. Not yet.

All illustrations are imperfect. Vancouver is not ideal; it rains a lot and feels dreary in January. The life of a believer after her soul has been torn from her body is not like that. Every illustration has limits to it, and mine certainly does. In contrast, the dead in Christ are now experiencing perfection. They have perfect joy, perfect fulfillment, gaze on exquisite glory, and behold the presence of the Father. But they are not yet experiencing the ultimate fulfillment. They, like us, await the renewal of all things. They long for the resurrection of their bodies and of the physical experience of Heaven that awaits them. We with them eagerly anticipate the Second Coming of Jesus. In this way, both we (the Church on earth) and they (the Church in Heaven) are filled with anticipation and hope, actively believing that all the promises of God are true. He will yet renew all things.

Having established a number of stages in our salvation, the first being our conversion and the second being the intermediate state, we might then wonder about both the millennial reign of Christ and the final new heavens and earth.

The Bible seems to indicate a period of a thousand years between the time in which Christ returns and the time in which He will establish a new Heaven and a new earth. There is only one place in the Bible in which this matter is referred to, Revelation 20:1–3: "Then I saw an angel coming down from heaven, holding in his hand the key to the bottomless pit and a great chain. And he seized the dragon, that ancient serpent, who is the devil and Satan, and bound him for a thousand years, and threw him into the pit, and shut it and sealed it over him, so that he might not deceive the nations any longer, until the thousand years were ended. After that he must be released for a little while."

If we skip forward to verses 7–8, we read, "And when the thousand years are ended, Satan will be released from his prison and will come out to deceive the nations that are at the four corners of the earth, Gog and Magog, to gather them for battle; their number is like the sand of the sea." After the millennium, the Lord consumes the enemies of God. Satan is thrown into the lake of fire, and all of humanity is raised to stand before the great white throne.

While the millennium is only mentioned in Revelation 20, the concept seems to find root in a number of Old Testament passages. For instance, Isaiah 65:20 says of the days to come, "No more shall there be in it an infant who lives but a few days, or an old man who does not fill out his days, for the young man shall die a hundred years old, and the sinner a hundred years old will be accursed." The idea of there being a time when no infant dies, and yet there is a person who lives a short life and dies at a hundred, can't refer to Heaven where no one can "live out their days," nor can it refer to any time in this sin-cursed creation.

The obvious solution to the Isaiah passage is that Christ will return to the earth at His Second Coming. With Him will come those He has given a new body to. Then, for a thousand years, Christ will physically reign over this earth from Jerusalem. Those who partake in the first resurrection will have received glorified, perfect bodies that will never die. They will live on the earth in these perfect bodies, ruling and reigning with Christ. Of those who remain on the earth but are unbelievers, it would seem that many turn to the Lord. After all, Jesus seems to be portrayed as physically reigning in Jerusalem. This period ends with a final battle in which unbelievers form an alliance with Satan. Then comes the end of this earth.

For many, this seems speculative and unbelievable. Are we really to imagine a time when the resurrected are on earth at the same time as people who have not yet received these new bodies? I would argue that is exactly what the Bible teaches.

Since this is not a study in eschatology, let's avoid a lengthy discussion here. However, there is a key point to be made. Those who have died in Christ along with those who remain on earth share a common hope and faith. It is of great comfort for believers who have seen believing loved ones die that this faith and hope still unites us. Death has not broken our spiritual bond. We not only desire the resurrection of the body, but we desire to rule and reign with Christ.

When the millennium comes to an end, Revelation 20:11 says, "Then I saw a great white throne and him who was seated on it. From his presence earth and sky fled away, and no place was found for them. And I saw the dead, great and small standing before the throne, and books were opened." According to Revelation, a great judgment will ensue in which everyone will be judged. But those whose names are written in the Book of Life will not be judged by what they have done, but rather by what Christ has done for them.

And then, when all these things have transpired, Revelation 21:1 says, "Then I saw a new heaven and a new earth, for the first heaven and the first earth had passed away, and the sea was no more."

With that comes the dawning of an entirely new era. It is the beginning of a new creation: a new earth and a new Heaven. And the redeemed—having been saved by Christ, entering into a state of blessedness in the intermediate state, receiving a resurrected body, and reigning with Christ for a thousand years—now watch in amazement. God makes all things new. He creates a new dwelling place. The new Heaven and the new earth are a stunning act of His creative genius. And then He invites all those who are His to enter into an adventure that is greater, grander, and more far-reaching than we had ever imagined.

This then is the adventure described in the rest of this book.

CHAPTER EIGHT

THE INTERMEDIATE STATE

Paul arrived in the Greek city of Athens during his second missionary journey. Although Athens at that time was not the most important city in Greece, it was the centre of Greek thinking in terms of religion and philosophy. As Paul is waiting for his missionary team to join him, "his spirit was provoked within him as he saw the city was full of idols" (Acts 17:16). Representations of gods and goddesses, a religious practice utterly condemned in the Bible and abhorrent to Jews, was abundant and central to Greek culture and thought.

Paul began a dialogue in that city. He found willing participants to engage in a process of reasoning regarding faith in Christ. He started in a synagogue but soon found himself in a marketplace. In that culture, this was the acceptable way of communicating ideas.

The afterlife: dueling worldviews

The marketplace that Luke mentions was most likely the Agora, a place where religious dialogue was common and welcome. Paul created such a stir in what he said that he was taken to the Areopagus. This was a place where famous trials were held in

Athens' past. Here the intellectual elite of the city asked him to give an account for himself and his teaching.

All was going well. People were engaged, willing to dialogue and wanting to hear more until, according to the account, Paul indicated that God had fixed a date wherein He would judge the world through the man He had appointed. He was of course referring to Jesus. Still, everyone was listening, intrigued. But then Paul said something that seemed incredible to the Greek mind: God had given assurance that this man, Jesus, will judge the world by raising Him from the dead. According to Luke's account of this event, when the leading intellectuals of Athens heard of the resurrection of the dead, some mocked him.

The modern reader of this ancient account might wonder why the mocking began at the mention of the resurrection. The idea of life after death was a well-accepted Greek belief. For instance, the famous incident of Socrates' death is recounted by his student, Plato. Plato said that when Socrates was forced to drink the deadly cup of hemlock, he had a happy disposition. He expected a joyous life after death. Most Greeks did.

What then brought about the mockery when Paul mentioned the resurrection of Jesus? The answer is quite simple: Paul's description of the resurrection centred on the bodily resurrection of Jesus. He would have described Jesus being crucified, laid into a tomb, and then raised bodily from the dead. His dead body was not only raised to life but transformed at the same time. His resurrection body was no longer subject to death, disease, or decay.

In contrast, Greeks were the ultimate dualists. They made a radical distinction between the body and the soul. In Greek thinking, the body was the prison house of the soul. Hence, bodily existence was inferior to pure spirit. A great many Christians today have a Greek, not a Christian, conception of life after death.

For Plato, the disciple of Socrates, there is a visible world and an invisible or spiritual world. He believed that the great creator created the soul of the universe. Furthermore, the highest part of the soul of man was made of the same substance as that of the universe. But Plato also taught that there is a part of the soul and the creation of the human body that had been created by and entrusted to younger gods. This lower aspect of the soul and of the physical world is inferior to pure spirit. For Plato, the body was the enemy of the soul. Upon death, the souls of wise men and philosophers who have purified themselves from the pollution of the body depart from bodily existence into pure spirit.

Plutarch, another famous Greek philosopher, carried this thought even further. The soul, he said, survives after the death of the body but must be purged of all that belongs to it. The soul must be reduced to mind or intellect alone, which is the highest part of the soul. Both Plato and Plutarch spoke of the body as the enemy of the soul. The body was conceived of as a sackcloth robe, a tomb. Some unworthy souls, they argued, sink beneath the stream into bodily materiality. For them, the vision of a physical Heaven is lost entirely.

This belief system helps us understand why, when Paul spoke of the bodily resurrection of Jesus, the Greek philosophers in Athens mocked. Body, flesh, and the physical realm were considered parts of the lower order of things. They were inferior. To argue that God demonstrated the authority of Jesus by raising Him from the death of the body was complete nonsense. This event in Athens presents the clash between the Hebraic/biblical worldview, and that of the Greeks.

John 1:14 says, "The word became flesh and dwelt among us, and we have seen his glory, glory as of the only Son from the Father, full of grace and truth." This verse expresses the very heart of the gospel. The most amazing event in all history, one of inexpressible beauty, is when the eternal Son clothed Himself in human flesh.

The Greeks would have been appalled. Flesh, they argued, is the lower level of existence we are trying to escape. And yet, 1 John 1:1,5 says, "That which was from the beginning, which we have heard, which we have seen with our eyes, which we looked upon and have touched with our hands, concerning the word of life . . . this is the message we have heard from him and proclaim to you..." In other words, the greatest and most wonderful thing that ever happened occurred in flesh and blood. It occurred in a real body with a head and a torso, arms, hands, and fingers, with sights and sounds. We are declaring, says John, not a spiritual ideal apart from matter, but rather that God stepped into the human story in flesh and blood. John thought this was so important that, in 1 John 4:2–3, he writes, "Every spirit that confesses that Jesus Christ has come in the flesh is from God, and every spirit that does not confess Jesus is not from God. This is the spirit of antichrist."

Why is so much made of the physicality of Jesus? Why are those who deny the full humanity of Jesus so thoroughly condemned? The answer is that this has everything to do with the God of the Bible. Even though God is not physical but is Himself pure spirit, He—out of His goodness—created a physical world. According to Psalm 19:1, the physical heavens declare the glory of God. According to Isaiah 43:7, the physical creation of human beings is for God's glory.

So, let's remember what the Bible teaches about the physical world and our own physical body.

And God said, "It is good."

According to Genesis 1:31, when God finished creating the world, He said, "It is very good." A lesser deity did not create this world. Instead, it was the great, omnipotent, all-wise creator who formed it and was pleased with what He had made. That theme keeps coming up in the Bible. According to Psalm 29:3, physical thunder is the voice of God. According to Romans 1, even if you have never had a Bible, you would know something about God simply by observing the creation. Yes, the heavens declare the glory of God.

But the glory of God is also seen in the creation of man. In Genesis 2:7, we read, "Then the LORD God formed the man of the dust from the ground and breathed into his nostrils the breath of life, and the man became a living creature." Unlike Greek thought, where the body is a lower level of existence, here the body is *essential* to our humanity. Theologian John Murray explains that we don't just have bodies, we are bodies. Scripture doesn't teach that our souls or spirits are made first and then placed into bodies; rather, our bodies are an integral part of who we are from the start, not just something tacked on.[12]

Why is it so important to review this data? Many Christians mistakenly think of Heaven as an entirely non-physical, spiritual realm. And the reason they think that is not because the Scripture has informed them in this view. Rather, they have unwittingly drunk at the well of Greek philosophy.

I have been at more than one graveside memorial service where the preacher has said that this is just this man's working clothes. It is not the real him. But is that really biblical?

The idea that we are simply a spirit in a box, so to speak, or that we are only genuinely and essentially ourselves in our spirits or souls, is unbiblical. As one "word/faith" preacher loved to say, "I am a spirit being who happens to live in a body." We are not. This view of essentially being a spirit being gives rise to the idea that when our spirits are torn from our bodies at death,

---

[12] *Collected Writings of John Murray,* John Murray. Banner of Truth Trust, 1982.

only then do we become our genuine selves. But this is not the hope of the resurrection.

The intermediate stage

Against this background of what it means to be human, we are still left with the conundrum of death. If death represents the tearing of our spirits from our bodies, and if the hope of the believer is the reuniting of body and spirit, how are we to understand the intermediate stage? How are we to think about our existence between death and the Second Coming of Christ, when we will receive our new bodies? We know Paul has taught us that the moment after we die is better by far, and so we do well to embrace this wonderful truth.

What happens to a believer immediately after he or she dies? For those of us who are facing the end of our lives now, this must become an important part of our thinking. And for those who have had loved ones pass on, they too need hope. Jesus gave that kind of hope to the thief who was hanging next to Him on the cross: "Today you will be with me in paradise" (Luke 23:43). We notice that Jesus said it would happen on that very day, not when He returned a second time.

The term "Paradise" is interesting because it speaks of a garden. Should we think of the intermediate state in physical terms?

The word "Paradise" is used in only two other places in the New Testament. We find it used 2 Corinthians 12:2–4. There, Paul uses it in terms of a vision: "I know a man in Christ who fourteen years ago was caught up to the third heaven—whether in the body or out of the body I do not know, God knows. And I know that this man was caught up into paradise - whether in the body or out of the body I do not know, God knows—and he heard things that cannot be told, which man may not utter."

There is much to consider in this passage, but let's consider only the use of the terms "Third Heaven" and "Paradise." Notice that Paul uses these terms synonymously. Third Heaven and Paradise are the same thing.

For Paul, the term "Heaven" can be used in three ways. He can speak about the First Heaven as simply the atmosphere over our heads. Then he can speak about the Second Heaven as the cosmos. This would include the place of the sun, moon, stars, and planets. Finally, he can speak of the Third Heaven as the dwelling place of God. Paul says that this is the same location as Paradise. Going back to Jesus's promise to the thief on the cross, He was promising him Paradise as the place where God dwells and makes His presence known.

The second reference to Paradise is found in Revelation 2:7, and is a part of the message Jesus gave to the church in Ephesus: "He who has an ear, let him hear what the Spirit says to the churches. To the one who conquers I will grant to eat of the tree of life, which is in the paradise of God."

The Tree of Life is first found in Genesis 2:9, one of the trees found in the Garden of Eden. Evidently, Adam and Eve had never eaten from that tree. After they were driven out of the garden, they were forbidden from ever re-entering it. Genesis 3:22 says, "Lest [the man] reach out his hand and take of the tree of life and eat and live forever." It would seem then that the Tree of Life in Paradise corresponds to either the same tree, or a similar one.

All of this is to say that when Jesus promised the thief on the cross that He would be with him in Paradise that day, He was promising him a garden in the presence of God where he would eat from a tree and live forever. Anyone dying in Christ today is promised the same thing. At the risk of being redundant, we are saying that no believer, upon death, goes into unconscious existence. Instead, they enter Paradise immediately.

2 Corinthians 12 contains Paul's description of his own experience of going into the Third Heaven. He says he does not know if that vision was in the body or out of it. That is to say, he is not sure whether he physically went there or whether he simply saw it in a vision. The experience was real enough, but later, as he is considering the experience, he does not know exactly how he experienced it. Could the intermediate state be something like Paul's experience?

For many Bible teachers, the intermediate state is an extraordinary period in our existence when we live without the body in Paradise. But unlike the experience of Paul, we are aware that we are without a body. But it is this idea of a disembodied spirit that has some of us concerned. How can such a thing exist? For one, it seems to resemble the Greek ideal rather than the biblical one. Secondly, one must wonder how it is possible for the soul to think and feel and act outside of the body. Up until death, the soul has known no existence apart from the body. Is it now to exist, even for a brief period, in a conscious fashion? And how are we to understand this consciousness?

What clues does the Bible give?

Paul says the state between our death and the receiving of our new bodies is far better than our state here in this fallen earth. And yet, some of us struggle to be convinced. Drifting about as a disembodied spirit seems to go against the very essence of the Bible's teaching on the importance of the body. After all, we are not a spirit who happens to have a body. We are, at all times, both physical and spiritual beings created by God to live for eternity.

What does the Bible teach about the intermediate state? Let's begin by admitting that we don't have the kind of clarity we might want. But we do have a clear teaching on the importance of the body and the physical realm. So, where do we start?

Perhaps we should go back to Jesus's parable of the rich man and Lazarus found in Luke 16:19–31. Notice several features about the story. First, the rich man died and was buried. Next, we encounter him in Hades where he is in torment. Then he looks at a distance and sees Abraham with Lazarus being comforted at his side. Finally, he calls out. He wants Lazarus to bring him water to cool his tongue. Does a disembodied spirit have a tongue? Is the spirit able to see as we see today?

If the parable is taken at face value, it seems to have all the marks of physical existence. The rich man sees with eyes and is complaining of physical anguish. He speaks with mouth about the longing for water on his tongue. But to this, many would argue, we press this parable to make it say too much. Clearly the point of the story is that after death both the righteous and the unrighteous become immediately aware of their eternal spiritual status. But does that necessarily mean that the status spoken of is physical? The parable of Luke 16 can be interpreted to speak of physical life. But others would understand these details as anthropomorphisms. That is, Jesus might simply be using easily understood physical language to convey the spiritual realities of the life to come.

Are there other hints of human experiences in the intermediate state? The Bible records several occasions in which people saw those who had died. One of those is recorded in 1 Samuel 28. This is the incident in which Saul calls on a medium to speak to the deceased prophet Samuel. The woman is afraid, for even though she does not know the king is before her, she does know that the king has forbidden mediums to operate in Israel. Nonetheless, she reluctantly agrees. The séance begins. To the woman's surprise, Samuel appears. Saul asks, "What does he look like?" She describes him: "He is an old man, and he is wrapped in a robe." The idea of a physical robe might not be surprising, but the idea that Samuel would appear physically old might strike us as surprising. Do we maintain our age at death in the intermediate period?

We might want to compare this account in 1 Samuel to the account described in Matthew 17. Jesus is on the Mount of Transfiguration with Peter, James, and John. There, the three disciples see Moses and Elijah talking with Jesus. In response to what they see, Peter suggests he make three tents for them. This seems to indicate that Moses and Elijah came bodily speaking with Jesus. At the very least, this is how the three men saw them.

Finally, we might also do well to consider the book of Revelation. John describes a scene in Heaven in which the righteous dead appear before Christ. They are described as awaiting the Second Coming of Jesus. We have to assume they are awaiting their final resurrection body. And so we should wonder what form of existence they are experiencing.

"When he opened the fifth seal, I saw under the altar the souls of those who had been slain for the word of God and for the witness they had borne" (Revelation 6:9). This is a depiction of the martyrs. They are pictured as being under the altar. This is significant, for the altar is the place of sacrifice. Having been sacrificed to God on an altar for their faith, they are being honoured by being allowed to dwell in this sacred place. But in reading this passage, the reader is immediately struck by the phrase "the souls of those." It is easy to conceive of these martyrs as having souls, but no bodies.

We have seen passages that seem to speak of the physicality of the intermediate state, and yet here we have a picture of souls with no reference to bodies at all. But we do well here to notice that Revelation 6:11 says, "Then they were each given a white robe and told to rest a little longer." The white robe is one of honour that marks their special place as martyrs. A robe, however, sounds physical. How does a disembodied soul wear an actual robe? Either the language of the soul or of the robe is symbolic. And because the book of Revelation has so many images, both real and symbolic, it is not always easy to detect how each image is to be understood. But it should be apparent that the picture of the souls under the altar cannot be used as objective evidence of disembodied spirits in Heaven.

But we can come to a certain conclusion. Whenever language is used to speak of those in the intermediate state, it always employs physical existence interacting with a physical environment. And that is entirely in line with what the Bible speaks of as the real essential nature of man.

The mystery of the intermediate state

In the end we will have to admit some agnosticism regarding this issue. Unlike our final state, the intermediate state is one that will remain shrouded in some mystery. Some will argue that, perhaps, Paul's experience of the Third Heaven is the best way to understand the intermediate state. The experience is real and physical, yet we are left to wonder if it is a vision or a real physical experience.

This discussion may be all that we can say. Some uncertainty about the nature of the intermediate state must be allowed to remain. However, we should not be quick to adopt the idea of disembodied spirits in Heaven. Perhaps Randy Alcorn is right when he suggests that God will design a temporary body for us.[13] However, I am not completely satisfied with his explanation. The idea of a temporary body leaves me with more questions than answers. Is it true that God assigns temporary bodies in Heaven? Are these bodies inferior to the final one we will receive? In what respects? Given that our new body in the new heavens and earth will be the self-same body that we had here (we will explain this later), is this body completely different? How so? Has God built

---

[13] *Heaven*, Randy Alcorn. Carol Stream, IL: Tyndale House Publishers, 2004

in some deficiencies into these heavenly bodies? As we can see, these questions are not easily answered.

I find it better to say that we experience life in a physical way in the intermediate state. But we, like Paul, may say that until the receiving of our new bodies we were never fully aware if we were in or out of the body.

The answer to the question of the nature of our experience in the intermediate state may prove to be more mysterious than we have yet grasped.

Human life is physical and spiritual rolled into one. And since the saints who die and enter the Lord's presence are portrayed in physical ways, it seems likely that is exactly how they experience life. After all, they are in the Garden of Paradise and invited to eat from the Tree of Life. The Bible describes them wearing robes and speaking with real mouths and tongues. But in His wise providence, God has so ordained it that the intermediate experience remains shrouded in mystery. It is a physical experience, to be sure, but it is not the final physical experience of which we eagerly await.

What should all of this say to us today? I believe we should not fear that at any time we will experience life in a disembodied fashion. For this reason, we must not fear death. Of course, it is true that these earthly bodies soon wear out and will be laid into the earth. And yet, we are assured that the moment the believer dies, he or she will enter Paradise. There they will see God, eat and drink, and wear clothing appropriate to the situation. Therefore, fellow believer, be content. God knows what you will need in Paradise. When you enter there, you will immediately say, "This is better by far!"

CHAPTER NINE

THE FINAL JUDGMENT

Let's briefly review what has been said. We have spoken about the ever-present reality of death. We have seen that Heaven is not our default position, and for this reason we need a Saviour. We have tried to define what happens to a human being at death. We have tried to understand the reality of the fate of those who have remained in a state of animosity toward God, and we have described the state of the believing dead in the intermediate state.

We have also described the states in the redemption of believers. First, we hear the Good News of Christ and believe. We are born again. At this time, the life to come, also called "eternal life," is already imparted into us. This is our foretaste of what is to come. If we should die before Christ returns, we will immediately be ushered into Heaven where we will be in the presence of the Lord. Even though the exact details of that life will remain a mystery until we experience it, we know that the intermediate state (when compared to the life we enjoy now) is better by far.

When Christ returns, the believers who have died in Him and are in the intermediate state will return with him from the heavens. They will immediately receive their final resurrection bodies. The believers who are left alive at Christ's return will receive their new bodies next. Then together, those who were dead and those who are alive will be caught up to be with the Lord.

We have also briefly made mention of the reality of the millennium, a period of a thousand years where those believers redeemed by Christ, with undying resurrection bodies, assist Him in His governance of the earth. At the end of the millennium, the earth and its elements will be dissolved (see 2 Peter 3:10). "The heavens will pass away with a roar, the heavenly bodies will be burned up and dissolved, and the earth and the works done on it will be exposed."

At that time, when the last chapter of this sin-cursed earth has been written, the Bible indicates the next great event:

> Then I saw a great white throne and him who was seated on it. From his presence earth and sky fled away, and no place was found for them. And I saw the dead, great and small, standing before the throne, and books were opened. Then another book was opened, which is the book of life. And the dead were judged by what was written in it. Death and Hades gave up the dead who were in them, and they were judged, each one of them, according to what they had done. Then Death and Hades were thrown into the lake of fire. This is the second death, the lake of fire. And if anyone's name was not found written in the book of life, he was thrown into the lake of fire. [Revelation 20:11–15]

There are some who argue that there are three separate judgments. From my understanding of Scripture, there is only one final judgment, happening at the same time and place. It will happen after the millennium and the rebellion that occurs at the end of it, resulting in Christ's final triumph.

The final judgment

The final judgment presents us with a picture of a righteous God who demonstrates His justice in the life of every human being. With the billions of people who have lived and died, not one life is forgotten. Not one deed done on this earth can be covered up, either the good or the bad. As Jesus said in Luke 12:3, "Therefore whatever you have said in the dark shall be heard in the light, and what you have whispered in private rooms shall be proclaimed on the housetops."

According to 2 Timothy 4:1, it is Jesus Christ Himself who is the judge of the living and the dead. That is repeated in Acts 10:42, where we are told that Jesus is the one who is ordained by God the Father to judge the living and the dead. That would mean that all who have died and all who remain at the end of the millennium will stand before Christ for judgment. In short, no one, including believers, will be excluded. But as Jesus indicates in Matthew 25:31–32, "When the Son of Man comes in his glory, and all the angels with him, then he will sit on his glorious throne. Before him will be gathered all the nations, and he will separate people one from another as a shepherd separates the sheep from the goats." We can see Jesus moving among the mass of humanity and arranging them into two groups, the redeemed and those who have no redeemer.

According to the 1 Corinthians 6:3, unbelievers, believers, and the angelic beings will be judged.

Revelation 20 states that when humanity stands before the throne, books are opened. John doesn't tell us what these books are, but the context seems to indicate that they contain the deeds of all people. These books will include an accurate record of what they have done, what they have left undone, what they have thought, and what they have loved and hated. They contain a full objective evaluation of every human life. According to Jesus in Matthew 12:36, "On the day of judgment people will give account for every careless word they speak." And Ecclesiastes 12:14 says, "For God will bring every deed into judgment, with every secret thing, whether good or evil."

From this it becomes clear that every human will be judged on the basis of their works. According to Romans 2:6, "He will render to each one according to his works." Later, in verse 11, we are told, "God shows no partiality." One's position in life, one's wealth, and whatever might have given a person an advantage in life, is all cleared aside. That might be what John means when he says that before this throne of judgment, earth and sky fled. He means that no other extenuating matters can be brought in. Of course, the earth has been burned up, and so all hope any person had in this earth perishes as well.

And what will be the result of these books? Romans 3:10 has already indicated God's judgment: "None is righteous—not one."

But judgment, it seems, does more than simply find everyone wanting. According to Romans 2:6, people are judged by what they have done. This helps us to see two important features of the final judgment. First, it helps us to rid ourselves of the mistaken notion that people are condemned because they didn't become Christians or because they rejected Christ. Instead, they will be condemned because of their deeds. Second, it also helps us to answer those who take issue with the final judgment, asking what happens to the person who has never heard of Christ. The answer is that every person will be judged by their works. This is reinforced in Romans 1, where Paul declares that the wrath of God is poured out because people suppressed even the truth of God that they had from nature. Judgment will be fair.

Jesus supplies us with everything we need to be spared from the devastating judgment to come. His rescue plan is found in His substitutionary death on the cross for His elect. But if this is so, is it not true that believers in Christ will not be judged on the basis of their works? To be clear, everyone will be judged on the basis of their works. Either the judgment will be on the basis of *our* works, or, should we surrender our lives to Christ the Saviour, the judgment will be on the basis of *His* works. The marvelous nature of our salvation is that when believers stand before the bar of God's judgment, all who believe will find that their lives are hidden in Christ.

Notice that because judgment is on the basis of works, punishment or reward is meted out on the same criteria. Jesus said, "And that servant who knew his master's will, but did not make ready or act according to his will, shall receive a severe beating. But he who did not know and did what deserved a beating, shall receive a light beating" (Luke 12:47–48). And in Matthew 11:22, Jesus tells the cities of Chorazin and Bethsaida that "it will be more tolerable on the day of judgment for Tyre and Sidon than for you." So we affirm that God's justice is not administered with a crude hammer. Rather, it is administered with the precision of a scalpel. It is tailor-made for every human being.

But what about believers? According to Revelation 20, another book is opened at the judgment, the Book of Life. Every once in a while we hear people say, "We will be surprised by who is in Heaven and who is not." Is this true? It may be so now, but it will not be true then. Let's be clear: scripture indicates that all those who died with their name in the Book of Life were immediately ushered into Paradise when they died. All who were left alive at the coming of the Lord, who had their names in the Book of Life, will be taken up in the twinkling of an eye and immediately receive their resurrection bodies. And so, in truth, by the time of the judgment before the great white throne, there will be no surprises at all. The mystery of who believed and who did not will have been resolved long before anyone arrives at the judgment. So why this opening of the Book of Life?

I think the answer is that it is an important act nonetheless. It is done to proclaim the work of Christ, a symbolic act. The opening of the Book of Life makes the statement that it contains a list of all who would have been condemned with the rest of mankind were it not for the saving work of Christ. The opening up of the Book demonstrates that the outcome of Judgment Day was in keeping with God's righteousness.

Since Christ was condemned on behalf of the redeemed, is there then no judgment for the saints? The answer is yes, there is! When Paul is speaking to believers in 2 Corinthians 5:9-10, he says, "So whether we are at home or away [that is, alive here on earth or having died in the intermediate state], we make it our aim to please him. For we must all appear before the judgment seat of Christ, so that each one may receive what is due for what he has done in the body, whether good or evil."

Hence, there is a judgment coming for all who name Christ. But what can this be, since the Bible makes it clear, according to Romans 8:1, that there is no condemnation for those who are in Christ Jesus?

The judgment of believers: for Christ's glory

We get hints about the judgment of believers from several passages in scripture. 1 Corinthians 3:12-15 records Paul speaking about the care that each of us should take as we build upon the foundation of Christ. In that passage, the foundation represents the fundamental truths about Christ, His gospel, the Church and the doctrines found in scripture. Now, says Paul, if we build on that foundation using substandard building materials, the final judgment day will disclose the kind of work we have done. Inspired by the Holy Spirit, Paul reveals there are some whose names are written in the Book of Life who will see that everything they have done in this life has amounted to no eternal benefit.

Other passages speak about this as well. In 1 Corinthians 4:3-5, Paul writes, "But with me it is a very small thing that I should be judged by you or by any human court. In fact, I do not even judge myself. For I am not aware of anything against myself, but I am not thereby acquitted. It is the Lord who judges me. Therefore, do not pronounce judgment before the time, before the Lord comes, who will bring to light the things now hidden in darkness and will disclose the purposes of the heart. Then each one will receive his commendation from God."

For those who are confused at this point, let's remember the totality of scripture. 1 Corinthians 4:3-5 speaks about a *commendation from* God, not a *condemnation for* God. Our sins were born by Christ, and we bear them no more. Even if it should be, as Paul teaches, that the Lord will bring to light all things now hidden in darkness, that should not disturb the believer.

Some believers find the prospect of a thorough examination of their lives to be troubling. They feel intimidated that their secret sins will be made known. But we should not fret. Let every sin we have ever done in life be exposed. Let everything that now shames us become known. The revelation of our sin will not serve to condemn us, it will only serve to highlight the grace of He who has taken away our condemnation. For it should, for the sake of His glory, be made known how great is the grace, love, and mercy of He who paid for our sins on His cross. If all our secret sins are made known, we will not be condemned. For Christ was condemned for us! Making our sins known will only serve to make us more aware of what Christ has done for us. It will highlight His glory, and we will worship Him.

But some will object. Doesn't Hebrews 8:12 say that "I will remember their sins no more"? Let's be clear about what that verse doesn't say: that God has amnesia, that there are huge gaps in His memory process, like a God with dementia. To never remember our sins is to say that God will never use them against us. He never calls them to mind in His judgment against us, for Christ has been judged on our behalf.

If that is the case, why are believers judged at all? The answer must be that the judgment of believers is a judgment unto rewards. So we are not to fear condemnation. Rather, Christ will judge the nature of the reward we will receive from His hands.

Judgment unto rewards

Where does the Bible teach this? We have already seen that Paul mentions that we must all stand before the judgment seat of Christ when each will receive His commendation, but not God's. But there is more. Consider Jesus's teaching on this matter, found in the Parable of the Ten Minas in Luke 19. A nobleman goes into a far country. While he is gone he calls ten of his servants, giving them each a *mina*, a unit of money. Each is told to engage in business until the nobleman returns. When he does, "The first came before him saying, 'Lord, your mina has made ten minas more'" (verse 16). In other words, he had earned a tenfold rate of return. And in response, the nobleman tells that man, "I will put you over ten cities." Another will be put over five cities. From this parable we learn that on the day of judgment, when Christ judges His own, He hands out rewards in keeping with the faithfulness of the servant. It is a judgment unto rewards. To some much is given. To others less is given.

This idea of rewards in Heaven is standard biblical teaching. In Matthew 5:11–12, Jesus says, "Blessed are you when others revile you and persecute you and utter all kinds of evil against you falsely on my account. Rejoice and be glad, for your reward is great in heaven." From Jesus's teaching we see that not only are there rewards, but some rewards, as we have seen, are larger than others.

Should the idea of receiving a reward in Heaven actually motivate us? Some find the thought of being faithful to the gospel to receive a greater reward in Heaven troubling. It appears to them that this is a lessor motive. Should not our reason be purely as a response of love for Christ without reference to what advantage we might receive because of it? None should deny that gratefulness for our salvation should motivate us to faithfulness.

However, Jesus Himself was motivated by rewards. Hebrews 12:2, speaking of Jesus, says, "Who for the joy that was set before him endured the cross, despising the shame, and is seated at the right hand of the throne of God." Jesus endured the cross, and not just because He obeyed the Father in all things. Of course, He was determined to submit to the Father in everything. But Hebrews tells us He was also motivated by the joy that awaited Him when He would be seated at the right hand of the Father.

Paul invites believers to do the same. In Colossians 3:23–24, he says, "Whatever you do, work heartily, as for the Lord and not for men, knowing that from the Lord you will receive the inheritance as your reward." Or consider 2 Corinthians 9:6, which speaks of the rewards granted to believers in the final day: "Whoever sows sparingly must also reap sparingly, and whoever sows bountifully will also reap bountifully." Matthew 10:41–42 agrees: "The one who receives a prophet because he is a prophet will receive a prophet's reward, and the one who receives a righteous person because he is a righteous person will receive a righteous person's reward. And whoever gives one of these little ones even a cup of cold water because he is a disciple, truly, I say to you, he will by no means lose his reward."

Over and over again, the Bible encourages us to strive to gain rewards that will not pass away. In Luke 12:33, Jesus even encourages His followers to make for themselves the kind of money belts that do not wear out. He then tells them they have an unfailing treasure in Heaven.

Since there are differing levels of rewards in Heaven, are there also differing levels of happiness? Jonathan Edwards wrote, "There are different degrees of happiness and glory in heaven. As there are degrees among the angels, viz. throne, dominions, principalities and powers; so, there are degrees among the saints. The glory of the saints will be in proportion to their eminency in holiness and good works here."[14]

But we might find that troubling. Wouldn't that create problems in Heaven? If one is put in authority over much and another over little, would this hierarchy not mirror the misery of competition and envy we find here on earth? Here again Jonathan Edwards helps us: "And there shall be no such thing as envy in heaven, but perfect love shall reign through the whole society. Those who are not so high in glory as the other, will not envy those that are higher, but they will have so great, and strong, and pure love to them, that they will rejoice in their superior happiness."[15]

We need to imagine a Heaven that is not static, but dynamic and growing. We need to imagine one where the saints will rule with Christ and be given varied and different assignments. But we need also to imagine a Heaven where the reward that comes is related to our faithfulness here. And we need to imagine a Heaven not besought with sorrow or disdain—a society where perfect love prevails.

---

[14] *The Works of Jonathan Edwards (Vol 2)*, Jonathan Edwards. Edinburgh: Banner of Truth Trust, 1974
[15] *Ibid.*

The life of Heaven is not disconnected to the life we live here on earth. This life is therefore meaningful. We need to be engaged in the Master's business, for the things we do in the name of Christ that redound to His glory will matter in eternity. If we shun the flesh, if we crucify it with its desires, and if we gladly, for the sake of Christ, suffer the loss of all earthly things, we will by no means lose our reward. We must see that the business of the saints is an eternal business. Unlike those who have no hope, we are involved in an eternal project.

CHAPTER TEN

A NEW HEAVEN AND A NEW EARTH

I wonder what you imagine when you think about going to Heaven? In a recent conversation with a fellow believer, she told me that as a little girl hearing about Heaven, she found the idea most unattractive. It seemed to her like a very long church service. Truth be told, in many of the popular images of Heaven it seems like an uninteresting place. When you get past the idea of endless golf courses and sitting on clouds playing harps, many people imagine a static existence where nothing new is ever invented or discovered. Perfection is a state where the same thing is repeated for eternity.

Whenever movies portray Heaven, it seems as though everything is white: the floor, the clothes, the walls, the furniture, and even the mist or clouds that cover the place to everyone's ankles. Where is the colour? Where are the rocky mountains? Where are the great waterfalls, the endless variety of creatures, the deserts, the lakes, and the eagles crying in the sky? Indeed, many popular descriptions of Heaven make our current world seem so much more attractive than that one. It isn't any wonder that so few of us dream and long for it. Some time ago I met a dying friend, a believer, in his room in the hospital. I asked him what his thoughts were of Heaven. He told me he had none. I marvelled at this. Although he loved Christ, there was nothing about Heaven that filled his imagination with anticipation. How tragic that so many are unfamiliar about what the Bible teaches of the life to come.

Furthermore, some of the things said about Heaven in theological circles should leave all of us scratching our heads and wondering what on earth they are talking about. Some people refer to Heaven less like an actual place and more like a state of mind. Heaven ceases to be a destination and becomes a condition! Imagine if someone talked that way about somewhere on earth. Here is an example: "I am from the Greater Vancouver area of British Columbia. What if I were to tell you that Vancouver is not so much a place, but a state of mind?" Wouldn't that kind of talk leave you with no concrete understanding of the city at all?

Is Heaven a real place?

The most basic question that needs to be addressed is about the existence of an actual place called Heaven. Let's consider the ascension of Jesus. He had not been raised in an abstract state of being, but physically. He spent forty days with His disciples. During that time He was eating with them, teaching them, and even on one occasion preaching to more than 500 at one time. After that time, according to Acts 1:9, "And when he had said these things, as they were looking on, he was lifted up, and a cloud took him out of their sight."

We have to imagine Jesus and His disciples on the Mount of Olives. He is giving the disciples their last instructions. He tells them not to leave Jerusalem until the Holy Spirit comes on them. And then He doesn't simply disappear or dematerialize and turn into a pure spirit. Neither does He go into some immaterial state called Heaven. He physically begins to rise into the air. As He keeps rising, He appears much smaller as the distance between Him and His disciples grows. Finally, a cloud takes Him out of their sight. What are the disciples to think about this? Exactly what you would think: *He is not dematerializing into another state, He is physically travelling to another place.*

Acts 1:10-11 says, "And while they were gazing into Heaven as he went, behold, two men stood by them in white robes, and said, 'Men of Galilee, why do you stand looking into Heaven? This Jesus, who was taken up from you into heaven...'" Again, to emphasize the point, the disciples would have thought He was physically going from one location to another. This is much like what we would do when we get onto an airplane and travel to another location. Our loved ones don't see us anymore, for we have travelled from one physical location to another.

Clearly, from the description of Jesus's ascension, He did physically travel from one place to another. However, it is important to define what this means. We are not saying that if you could take a spaceship you could get there from here. It is important to say this because some have suggested that one should be able to observe the constellations through a high-powered telescope and guess the exact location of Heaven. It seems more than likely that Heaven exists in some other dimension. But stating matters in that fashion should not lead to the conclusion that Heaven is any less physical or real than our experience of the present creation. Even though at present Heaven can't be perceived with our physical senses, we should think of it as in some physical geographical location.

Let's clear away some difficulties that we might entertain. We know that because Jesus is fully God, He is omnipresent. By that we mean that He is present in all places at all times. That is why, for instance, John 1 records Him saying to Nathaniel, that "Before Philip called you, when you were under the fig tree, I saw you" (verse 48). Even in His incarnation, when Jesus the eternal Son takes on human flesh, He never ceases to be the ever-present, omnipresent God. But in His humanity, He is physically and bodily present somewhere. That is to say, He is bodily present in a real place.

Consider Jesus's words in John 14:2 to His disciples spoken during the last supper: "In my Father's house are many rooms," or dwelling places, or many mansions. He refers to a place where a traveller might spend a night, or a place where a wealthy individual might have a villa in which he lived. Anyone hearing those words from Jesus had concrete images of a physical location where they could remain: "In my Father's house are many rooms. If it were not so, would I have told you that I go to prepare a place for you?" (John 14:2). Notice He doesn't declare, *I go to prepare a state of mind for you*. He is referring to an actual physical place that exists somewhere in a real location.

Once we settle on the picture of an actual physical place, we never again fall prey to the idea of some obscure spiritual dimension devoid of anchor points. This is a location that is being prepared to receive a vast number of inhabitants.

New heavens and new earth

But what else do we know? We know that this place is not just called "Heaven." Fascinatingly enough, the Bible speaks of a new Heaven, and then it speaks of a new earth. God has made a promise: "For behold, I create new heavens and a new earth; and the former things shall not be remembered" (Isaiah 65:17). Isaiah repeats this promise again in the next and last chapter of his book. "For as the new heavens and the new earth that I make shall remain before me, says the LORD, so shall your offspring and your name remain" (Isaiah 66:22). Here is the promise that the new heavens and the new earth will endure forever. Furthermore, we are also promised that God's people will live forever there. So, are the new heavens and earth the place where we will eternally remain, never moving?

Before we answer that, notice that the phrase "new heavens and new earth" is not only used in Isaiah—Peter also uses it: "But according to his promise we are waiting for new heavens and a new earth, in which righteousness dwells" (2 Peter 3:13). In other words, that is our eternal hope. The phrase is also used in Revelation 21:1, where John takes us to the scene after the great judgment of the nations: "Then I saw a new heaven and a new earth, for the first heaven and the first earth had passed away, and the sea was no more."

Notice that the words "the sea was no more" has led some Bible teachers to imagine that, in the world to come, there will be no oceans. Perhaps, but perhaps not. On the one hand, the mention of the seas is to be compared to earlier passages that describe the antichrist arising out of the turbulent seas. The seas in Revelation 21 might refer to the nations that are ever in rebellion against their Creator. But the sea might also refer to something else. Remember that in the world in which John lived, the sea presented an uncrossable barrier. Most shipping was done within sight of land. Sailors would use the landforms to keep fixed navigational reference points. It may be that John is describing a time to come when the uncrossable barrier between Heaven and earth is no more.

This is unlike our present reality. We know that at present there is no way for us to travel from earth to Heaven. There is currently a great gulf between us and the dwelling place of God. There is a sea that separates us from that realm. But in the time to come, this uncrossable barrier to the dwelling place of God no longer exists.

That leads us back to the first phrase in Revelation 21:1: "Then I saw a new heaven and a new earth." What can those words mean? And where is our eternal dwelling place?

Part of the puzzle of what the new earth refers to is answered in 2 Peter 3. In verse 6, Peter speaks about the world that once existed before the flood. In his words, that world was deluged with water and perished. Or, as Peter describes it, that world died. In the next verse Peter adds, "But by the same word the heavens and earth that now exist are stored up for fire, being kept until the day of judgment and the destruction of the ungodly" (verse 7). In verses 11-12, Peter writes of the heavenly bodies passing away with a roar. They will be burned up and dissolved.

Many biblical scholars have debated the meaning of this. Does it mean that this earth will be completely destroyed, much like a house in a fire? In that case, the earth as it now exists will be permanently destroyed. But others, while they admit the destruction of this earth, argue that there will be a renewal of this very same earth. One Bible teacher said, "God hangs on to his fallen original creation and salvages it. He refuses to abandon the work of his hands." Indeed, we might argue that He has sacrificed His own Son to save His original project. That would mean that this present earth is not temporary. Paul seems to indicate exactly that when he writes, "The creation itself will be set free from its bondage to corruption and obtain the freedom of the glory of the children of God" (Romans 8:21). Just like we are redeemed, so also will this earth be.

But what about Peter's vision of the heavenly bodies passing away with a roar, being burned up and dissolved? That seems to indicate a complete and utter destruction of this present earth.

And yet, in Jesus's Sermon on the Mount, He says, "Blessed are the poor in spirit for theirs is the kingdom of heaven" (Matthew 5:3). Two verses later He says, "Blessed are the meek, for they shall inherit the earth." He says it as if it is our destiny. We remember the promise of God found in Numbers 14:21, that the earth shall be filled with the glory of God. Is this the eternal future of the earth?

How do we put these two seemingly contradictory ideas together?

Imagine Jesus's body stepping out of the tomb. Is it a new body, or is it His old one? On the one hand, it has to be new because His old body was tortured, mutilated, and killed. As He steps out of the tomb, He does so not in weakness but in glorious strength. His resurrection body is eternal. But on the other hand, it has to be His old body. After all, where else would it be? It is not in the tomb. It has been raised to life. It didn't dematerialize. It didn't continue to decay. Furthermore, His body still bears the marks in His hands and feet from His crucifixion. He shows these things to demonstrate that it is really Him. And yet it is a new body. The lines of pain and weakness and subjection to sorrow have all permanently gone. That is why the disciples recognized Him and at the same time struggled to believe it was Him. In truth, the physical body of Jesus had been transformed into a body that was not subject to death or to dishonour. It was eternal, perfect.

That, I think, is the same image we should employ when we think about the new earth. In Romans 8:21 we are told that the creation will be set free from its bondage to corruption. This means it will be freed from the effects of sin. Then, in verse 23 of the same chapter, we are told that not only the creation, but we also will experience the redemption of our bodies.

Therefore, we must imagine the life to come. When Christ returns, we must imagine the believers who are on earth. In the twinkling of an eye, they are transformed. Their earthly bodies are redeemed and made new. They are made perfect, never to suffer decay. But what of believers who have already died and were buried? For most, their bodies will have been utterly destroyed. We will investigate this matter further in a later chapter. But it is clear that Christ raises up the bodies of those who have died and whose bodies have decayed, and in some way reunites these self-same bodies with their souls.

Since Romans declares that both our bodies and the earth will be redeemed, it seems to me that even after this earth is destroyed by fire, as Peter describes it, God raises the earth again, redeeming it. It is delivered from its bondage to decay. It is raised again, just like the dead body of Jesus.

We believe there will be a new earth, which will be this one. But we also believe this earth will be transformed in such a way that the curse, the fall, the limitations, and the things that bring death and alienation from God are gone. In the days to come we will live on this earth resurrected.

But what are the new heavens? Is Heaven, the dwelling place of God, also to be renewed? That would seem impossible, because Heaven was never subject to decay.

In 2 Corinthians 12:2 Paul speaks about Heaven, and there are three different ways to think about what he means. He can mean Heaven as in the atmosphere over our heads, or he can mean Heaven in reference to the cosmos. He can mean Heaven in reference to the dwelling place of God. Not only does Paul speak that way, but other Bible writers do as well. So, when Revelation 21:1 speaks of a new Heaven, we should note that it is not speaking of the dwelling place of God, but rather of the cosmos. This is the heavens in the sense of what we call *space*. The heavens are the sun, the moon, the stars, the planets, and the galaxies that make up our universe. So when John says he saw a new Heaven and a new earth, he means he saw a new universe or a new created order. All had been renewed and redeemed. And when he says there was no longer any sea, he means that the barrier that keeps this created order from the dwelling place of God has been removed. There is now a clear accessibility from this present order to the very throne room of God.

The holy city

We are then shown the next thing about the new creation in verse 2: "And I saw the holy city, the new Jerusalem coming down out of heaven from God, prepared as a bride, adorned for her husband" (Revelation 21:2). The New Jerusalem comes down from the dwelling place of God to earth. What can that mean?

We know that David captured Jerusalem from the Jebusites in around 1010 BC and it became the capital of the people of God. The name Jerusalem means "city of peace," but it has been anything but that. From my understanding, Jerusalem has been attacked fifty-two times and captured and recaptured forty-four times. It has seen unending wars, not peace.

And yet this is the city that both Psalm 46 and 87 call the "City of God." Psalm 48 calls it the "joy of the whole earth." Nehemiah, Daniel, and Isaiah call it the "Holy City." Psalm 50 calls it the "perfection of beauty." Psalm 46:4 calls it "City of God," and the "habitation of the Most High." That is because the temple was built there, and it became the centre of worship. It is also the city where our Lord was crucified.

But the city also has an eternal destiny. According to Hebrews 12:22-23, "But you have come to Mount Zion and to the city of the living God, the heavenly Jerusalem, and to innumerable angels in festal gathering, and to the assembly of the firstborn who are enrolled in heaven." This vision of Jerusalem is of a city that has no temple. It needs no temple, for the Lord himself is no longer veiled in that place. His light so illumines it that it needs no sun, it has the radiance of the glory of God with beautiful ornate walls built of jasper, while the city is pure gold that is as clear as glass. This Holy City is everything that the old Jerusalem hoped for but never became. This new Holy City comes down and touches the earth.

In some fashion, the boundaries between Heaven and earth have been breached. And just in case we are still wondering if this is an actual physical place, the exact dimensions of the place are given. I have always remembered its measurements in this way: it is about as long as from Vancouver to Winnipeg, and just as wide and high. If you can't get that image, it is about 1400 miles, or 2200 kilometres, long, wide, and high.

In Ephesians 1:10, we read that God's plan for the fullness of time is to unite all things in Christ—things in Heaven and on earth. Think of it this way: when Jesus became man, He never ceased to be God. He is fully God and fully man.

Now then, Heaven is the dwelling place of God. Earth is the dwelling place of man. Jesus Christ, the perfect God-man, forever brings together Heaven and earth. Yes, we live on the new earth for eternity, with sights and sounds and smells and mountains and plains and waterfalls and eagles crying in the heavens. It is a physical dwelling place. But it is different. The New Jerusalem has come down to earth and the gates of that city are never closed. The righteous nations of the earth bring their glory into the city.

I see, in the promise that God has given, a life to come where all the nations of the earth, redeemed by Christ's blood, live life with joy. There is no sorrow, no dying or pain. But the life to come is physical, with genuine human cultures replete with food and creativity, all for the glory of God. And in their joy of what the Father has done, the nations regularly enter the City of God to worship the great King.

There are so many more questions to address. What kind of a body do we have? What will we be doing? What will mark our worship? What does it mean to see God? Will we know everything, or will we learn new things? Keep reading.

CHAPTER ELEVEN

THE RESURRECTION OF THE BODY

The human body is a marvel. It is beautiful. It is complex and functional. It expresses who we are. Every human body consists of a number of biological systems. The circulatory system moves blood, nutrients, oxygen, carbon dioxide, and hormones through the body. The digestive system allows the body to break down and absorb food and remove waste. The endocrine system consists of eight major glands that secrete hormones into the blood. The immune system is the body's defense against disease. The lymphatic system also fights disease and helps the body combat infection. The nervous system controls voluntary and involuntary actions. The muscular system provides power to move and includes 650 muscles. The reproductive system, the skeletal system, the respiratory system, the urinary system, and even the skin itself protect the body from the outside world.

And all of that wonder is just the beginning. Human bodies have five vital organs: the brain, heart, kidneys, liver, and lungs. The human body consists of 100 trillion cells. We take 20,000 breaths every day. The human brain has about 100 billion nerve cells, and the complexity and interconnectedness of this organism is surely an example of God's wonderful feat of engineering. It is no wonder that Psalm 139:14 says, "I praise you, for I am fearfully and wonderfully made. Wonderful are your works; my soul knows it very well."

And yet, as we all know, this complex and wonderful body is subject to disease, aging, degradation, and death. Furthermore, on this side of the fall of Adam, our bodies can also be used in dishonourable ways. We employ the body's wonders in ways that sin against our Creator.

The Good News of the Bible is that when Christ brought salvation and redemption to us, He did not just save our souls, He came also to redeem our bodies. Our souls and bodies will be set free from all the results of the curse.

The redemption of our bodies

It always amazes me that, in spite of so much Bible teaching on the matter, there are still Christians who believe that the life to come is some kind of spiritual existence that does not resemble an actual physical, bodily existence. Many still envision disembodied spirits. They do this in spite of all the biblical material that describes exactly the opposite.

So, what will life be like in Heaven? We know about the new Heaven and earth, and then the dwelling place of God coming to the earth. The barrier between God and man is permanently removed. We also know that the world to come is a physical reality. It is a real place with sights and sounds and smells and tastes. But all of this needs to be set into a context. We cannot imagine our place in such a world if we do not have a bodily existence for all of eternity.

But that seems strange. Does my spirit simply get put into a new body in the age to come? What is it that I am actually to experience? According to *The Westminster Confession of Faith*, "All the dead will be raised up, with the self-same bodies, and none other." Have a look at your body. Stare at your face in the mirror. Look at your hands and your feet. Then say to yourself, 'This very body will go on for eternity.'"

Are you disappointed? Some will protest and say, "I was looking for something better than I had." But don't react too quickly. Let's not get ahead of ourselves. Is it true that we will have the self-same body in eternity that we have today? Is that just one opinion held by the authors of *The Westminster Confession*? Do others say the same?

In his *Systematic Theology*, Wayne Grudem says, "When Christ returns and raises from the dead the bodies of all believers for all time who have died, he reunites them with their souls, and changes the bodies of all believers who remain alive."[16] Before we ask what kind of change Grudem has in mind, let's agree that some kind of a change is necessary. Our present bodies are both a marvel of the engineering of our Creator and a fitting picture of the effects of the fall. We are both fearfully and wonderfully made, but also beset by great weaknesses. Such is the nature of our bodies on this side of the fall.

In his book *Heaven*, Randy Alcorn discusses the new body at length. He says, "When we die, it isn't that our real self goes to the intermediate Heaven and our fake self goes to the grave; it's that part of us goes to the intermediate Heaven and part goes to the grave to await our bodily resurrection. We will never be all that God intended for us to be until body and spirit are again joined in resurrection."[17]

Alcorn believes that in the intermediate state there is some kind of an intermediate body. We have discussed this matter in chapter 8. Whether this theory is true is not the issue. What is of key importance is that the new heavens and the new earth will go hand in hand with the reuniting of our souls to our bodies.

---

[16] *Systematic Theology*, Wayne Grudem. Zondervan & Inter-Varsity, 1994.
[17] *Heaven*, Randy Alcorn. Carol Stream, IL: Tyndale House Publishers, 2004

But that sounds strange and impossible. Once our bodies die, they are buried or cremated, or destroyed in some kind of accident. I live in British Columbia, where it rains constantly. The graves of those who are buried in this climate will soon see all vestiges of the body destroyed in a very short period. It seems that the reuniting of our souls with our bodies is a scientific impossibility. Once our bodies leach into the soil, nothing remains of them. How can this self-same body be reunited with a soul? And furthermore, what is the biblical evidence that this should be the case?

In order to understand this apparent impossibility, we begin with the resurrection of Jesus. 1 Corinthians 15 contains Paul's lengthy discussion of both the resurrection of Jesus and those who hope in Him. He states, "But in fact Christ has been raised from the dead, the first fruits of those who have fallen asleep" (1 Corinthians 15:20). The concept of a first fruit comes to us from the Old Testament. Leviticus 23:9–14 describes it. The feast of firstfruits happened at the beginning of the barley harvest. Because barley was the first crop reaped from the winter sowing, it represented the very first of all the harvest that lay before the people. It was a celebration that anticipated that, in this time of harvest, God would be faithful and provide Israel with an abundance of food for the rest of the year. That, says 1 Corinthians 15:20, is what the resurrection of Jesus is. It is the first of the harvest that anticipates a great harvest of resurrections to follow. Those coming resurrections will be just like the resurrection of Jesus.

Another way of stating this is to say that Jesus's resurrection from the dead is the prototype, or the first of all resurrections that follow Him. All coming resurrections will look just like His. And if that is the case, we should notice that it was His own body that was raised. Jesus's body did not rot in the grave, and He did not receive a new one. It was indeed His old body that was raised. We might add that it was His old body that was redeemed. And that is exactly what we should anticipate.

In 1 Corinthians 15:35–53, Paul explains in great detail exactly what it is we are to anticipate when we receive our resurrected bodies. He begins by giving us an illustration from nature: "But someone will ask, 'How are the dead raised? With what kind of body do they come?' You foolish person! What you sow does not come to life unless it dies. And what you sow is not the body that is to be, but a bare kernel, perhaps of wheat or of some other grain. But God gives it a body as he has chosen, and to each kind of seed its own body" (1 Corinthians 15: 35–38).

The illustration is an analogy. Just as seed thrown into the ground seems to die and be dissolved by the soil, it still produces a harvest, and so it is with the death of our own bodies. The analogy is interesting. On the one hand, the seed that is put into the ground ceases to exist in its original form. On the other, there is surely a connection between that form of the seed and what comes after it. So also the body that we sow into the ground and dies will not be recovered in the same form it was in before. There is a difference between the original and final form.

Having given the analogy, Paul explains that God designs all bodies for a specific function in mind: "For not all flesh is the same, but there is one kind for humans, another for animals, another for birds, and another for fish" (1 Corinthians 15:39). The point is that God creates different kinds of bodies. As He does so, each body He creates is created to function with a specific purpose in mind.

With regard to the resurrection of our own bodies, Paul explains that when our earthly forms are planted into the ground at our death, it is this self-same body that will be raised to life. But it will not be exactly like it was before, because God designs each body with a function in mind.

Paul now draws this discussion to its conclusion: "So it is with the resurrection of the dead. What is sown is perishable;

what is raised is imperishable. It is sown in dishonour; it is raised in glory. It is sown in weakness; it is raised in power. It is sown a natural body; it is raised a spiritual body" (1 Corinthians 15:42–44). And then he says, "As was the man of dust, so also are those who are of the dust, and as is the man of heaven, so also are those who are of heaven. Just as we have borne the image of the man of dust, we shall also bear the image of the man of heaven" (Verse 48–49).

God designs a body for the life to come

We who are still alive bear the image of the man of dust. Adam was created from the dust of the earth. As God created him, He perfectly designed him for life lived on the earth He had created for him. Originally his body was created so that it would never die. But Adam sinned, and with that sin he brought the seeds of death into his body. But the new heavens and earth will not be a land of death. Hence, it is necessary for God to design a body that perfectly fits the environment to come.

Realizing that each body is created by God for its purpose, Paul then makes a final statement: "I tell you this, brothers: flesh and blood cannot inherit the kingdom of God, nor does the perishable inherit the imperishable" (verse 50).

Imagine for a moment what it must have been like for Moses while he was on Mount Sinai. He asks God to see him as He is. God says, "You cannot see my face and live." To stand before His full glory would be like standing at ground zero of a nuclear blast. Moses's body was not created for it. Therefore, all that Moses would be allowed to see was the fading glory of God as He passed by. But, says Paul, God will take and renew the present body and make it fit for Heaven and the presence of God.

What then will our resurrection body be like? What will we be like in the life to come? Clearly we will have a body just like Jesus's raised one. We have already seen that His resurrection is a prototype of our own. That would mean that we would have, just like Jesus, a head, torso, arms, legs, fingers, toes, and so forth. Jesus looked human in every way we do today. And so we know with certainty that in the life to come we will be every bit as human as we are today. And yet Paul has reminded us that our present body cannot inherit the kingdom of God. Our bodies simply were not designed for it, even as a fish's body was not designed to fly.

What will our bodies be like?

How then will we be different from what we are today? First, whereas we are now subject to death, we will be imperishable.

The idea of being imperishable means that we will never wear out, never be sick, never have a cold or headache, or be subject to cancer. There will be no susceptibility to a global pandemic in the body to come. That is to say, the environment to come will not threaten our physical frame in the way the present environment does.

Furthermore, the body that is to be will not have weaknesses or physical handicaps. We won't struggle with our weight problems anymore—hallelujah! It seems amazing to think it, but the body to come will not grow old or show any of the signs of aging. Will we look youthful? I expect so, although I find no biblical statement about that matter. I suppose all we have here is our imagination of what will be, but it seems likely that all the physical characteristics of our present body will still be there with all our recognizable features. Even as Jesus was recognized after His resurrection, so also will we recognize each other. But it seems likely that we will display youthfulness and maturity at the same time. All that is to re-emphasize that the body to come is imperishable.

Second, whereas we are now subject to dishonour, we will be glorious.

There are several features to be considered here. 1 Corinthians 15:40 seems to describe the beauty of the body to come. I have often wondered what Adam and Eve must have physically looked like before the Fall. I can only imagine that now, after the Fall, the most beautiful or handsome human being bears but a pale resemblance to the splendour and magnificent beauty that shone from them. Is it possible then that our physical bodies in the world to come will outshine the beauty of the first human pair? That seems likely.

When Paul uses the term "glory," he always relates it to God. I think Paul means that our future bodies will reflect properly and perfectly all that the image of God was intended to reflect. We were created to accurately reflect the perfections of God's nature. One of the things that attracts me personally about the glorious body that is to come is the assurance that it will always honour God. Many times in this life, even in our best moments, we are aware there has never been a time when we were free from some self-centred motive. Even while the Bible commands that we do all things in faith, the Holy Spirit reveals that this has never been the case, even among the most holy of us. But as we exist with perfect bodies, everything we do—whether in the words we speak or in the things we give ourselves to do or create or build—will be fully for the glory of God. Mixed motives will be forever banished. All we do will accurately reflect the God who made us.

Third, whereas we are now subject to weakness, we will then be powerful.

This may seem redundant. After all, we already know that we are imperishable. What more can be said? But the idea of power contains the promise of strength. Recently I have had a great deal of pain in my feet and joints. I went to the doctor about it. She told me that, even though it was sore, I should keep walking every day. Following her advice, I walked in spite of pain. That was important. My doctor said, "You don't want to lose muscle strength." Eventually I overcame it and the pain retreated. I was thankful. But I was also reminded of my inherent weaknesses. However, the body to come will never fail to accomplish all it was designed to do. There will be enough strength to do what God intends for us.

The body to come will not be omnipotent. This would mean we would possess infinite strength. Omnipotence is an essential attribute of God. We might also call this an "incommunicable attribute." That is, omnipotence is unique to God. No other being will ever possess that which God alone possesses. Furthermore, we don't become God in eternity. Although the Bible says that we will be like God, it means it only in the sense that, as image-bearers of God, we will reflect the image of God exactly as we were intended. It is only in the world of paganism and polytheism that human beings become gods. The Bible makes it plain that both in eternity past and future there is but one God. We are not destined to be gods in our own right. That was the lie that Satan used to entice Eve, but it is not one that we claim for ourselves.

It is for that reason that we will have power, but not infinite amounts of it. Rather, we will have just enough to do what God assigns to us. I assume we will write books in Heaven, create art, build buildings, and study the natural properties of the new heavens and earth. In short, I have no doubt that human creativity will seek to know and engage in the understanding of the science of the new creation. We will engage in human activities, even as we have done so here. However, we will do these things to the glory of God, without mixed motives. None of the works of our hands and minds in the world to come will be stained with rebellion. Instead, I assume we will urge each other on to greater heights, always looking to reflect on the glory of the God who has made us so splendidly.

We should not imagine that the life to come is static. I don't believe we will know everything in Heaven. I believe we will become fully human. The nature of the human experience is to know our limitations. But the power of the new body means that weariness, laziness, depression, or simply the blues will affect us no more. There will be no disparity between what we want to do and what we do. It is a future of consistency.

Fourth, as we are now a natural body, we will become a spiritual body.

At first reading this might make us think that the body to come is not physical at all, but by now we should be ready to discount this. After all, it is still called a "body." We were created by God, after His image, with body and soul. It is therefore consistent with God's nature and work to grant us new resurrected bodies for eternity. The weakness of our present body is that we are often responsive to what Paul calls the "desires of the flesh." These most often refer to the habitual sinful patterns within us that are directed by the flesh. In this present life, there are times when we tell ourselves that we will not break out in anger as we did before, only to find ourselves doing it anyway. That is because the desires of the flesh overwhelm the desires of the mind. The body sometimes militates against the will.

But in the age to come, this will never be the case. What we intend to do will be what we do. The body will co-operate perfectly with the desires of the Holy Spirit so that we will live and act in a way that glorifies God at all times.

Fifth, whereas now we physically bear the image of Adam, we will then physically bear the image of Jesus.

This does not mean we are all going to look exactly like Jesus so that there will be no individuality among us. Instead, we will bear some of the unique characteristics of what we looked like here so that we will indeed recognize one another. But we shall be like Christ, with His desires.

I conclude that the writers of *The Westminster Confession* were right in saying that the self-same bodies are raised in the resurrection. By using the phrase "self-same," they did not mean that these bodies with their weaknesses will go on forever. What they meant was that the bodies we presently have will be transformed. That is, these self-same bodies are transformed. In some fashion, as Job said, "After worms have destroyed my body, yet in my flesh, I will see God."

But what do we make of the reality of these present bodies decaying in the ground at death? How can these bodies, which will one day not exist, be made new? Some have argued that God will "re-assemble" all the scattered elements of this body at the resurrection. Perhaps. We are not told. But we do know that God created all physical matter out of nothing. Go out and look at the world of nature. Its beauty and complexity are on display. But nature also proclaims the reality of a miracle. There is not a scientific principle that would bring something out of nothing into existence. However, this is the nature of our God. He simply speaks and all physical matter springs to life. It is for this reason, not a difficulty for God, that He should also speak in the new heavens, and all the disassembled bodies of the saints would be re- assembled at His command. After all, we are not looking for the life to come to arise out of our hope in the scientific principles of this world. Our hope has always been in the promise of a God who cannot but keep His word.

Our present bodies are fearfully and wonderfully made. How carefully God knitted us together in our mothers' wombs. How complex and wise is His creation of my frame. If that is true now, what can that mean when this very body is transformed?

The life to come is in some sense the life we now understand. It is a physical life. But it is more. It is the life we long for. It is the nature of being made in the image of God that all human beings long for a life that is full of plans and adventures. We long for a life that is ever aware of the loving hand of our God and Creator. But so much is presently lacking. Why is it, we ask, that we long for that which we have never seen? At our conversion, had we not already received eternal life?

CHAPTER TWELVE

SEEING GOD FACE TO FACE

The Bible teaches us about the new heavens and the new earth, and about the resurrection of the body. It also presents us with a picture of a real country with sights, sounds, smells, and tastes. We are told we will eat and drink in Heaven. We are told about a body not subject to weakness, aging, or disease.

But all of this pales in significance to the one thing that towers above all others: Heaven is the dwelling place of God. Revelation 22:3–5 says, "No longer will there be anything accursed, but the throne of God and of the Lamb will be in it, and his servants will worship him. They will see his face, and his name will be on their foreheads. And night will be no more. They will need no light of lamp or sun, for the Lord God will be their light, and they will reign forever and ever."

Satisfaction in God

Martin Luther once said, "I had rather be in Hell with Christ, than be in Heaven without him." Does that sound surprising? Psalm 73:25 says, "Whom have I in heaven but you? And there is nothing on earth I desire besides you." Of course, Luther did not believe he would be in Hell with Jesus. He did, however, believe that to be without Jesus would be the ultimate horror. And Asaph was not saying in Psalm 73 that there weren't things in nature that also gave him joy. He is saying that, in comparison to all other things, there simply is no competition between them and God. What he really wanted out of Heaven was not the body that will never tire, although he surely would have rejoiced in that news. Still, if you offered to give him that but did not give him God, he would not have been interested. Paul would say of his ancestry, "I count everything else as rubbish in order that I might gain Christ." This is the abiding passion of all who truly believe.

Psalm 84:1-2 says, "How lovely is your dwelling place, O LORD of hosts! My soul longs, yes, faints for the courts of the LORD; my heart and flesh sing for joy to the living God." Then, in verse 10, the psalmist adds, "For a day in your courts is better than a thousand elsewhere. I would rather be a doorkeeper in the house of my God than dwell in the tents of wickedness."

In contrast, there are all manner of people who seek Heaven but do not seek God. They have passions in their lives that do not include God. Some passions are not necessarily bad on their own, but they do not seek God as their highest joy. They know so little about what David spoke about in Psalm 27:4: "One thing have I asked of the LORD, that will I seek after; that I may dwell in the house of the LORD all the days of my life, to gaze upon the beauty of the LORD and to inquire of his temple."

Most have no understanding of what Moses said to God after He told him that he would lead him and the people to the Promised Land. In Exodus 33:15, Moses says, "If your presence will not go with me, do not bring us up from here." Imagine saying, "If your presence is not in Heaven, then Lord, don't bring me up to there!" What all these people from scripture are saying is that they have no greater desire than to gaze on God's beauty. Indeed, Heaven will have no inhabitants that do not agree!

Years ago, John Piper wrote a ground-breaking book entitled *Desiring God*.[18] In it, he wants to correct hedonistic America for not being hedonistic enough! Our society settles for short-term pleasures and ignores the ultimate pleasure of knowing God. We are like children, making mud pies when there is a feast from God before us. In that same book, Piper would go on to say that God is most glorified in us when we are most satisfied in Him.

And it is this satisfaction in God, this delight in Him, this finding in Him the sole source of all pleasure and the reason for existence, that is the fountainhead of all that is lovely. The consummation of all we have longed for is that which makes the redeemed long for Heaven. Perhaps that is exactly what Paul meant when he said that to depart and be with Christ is better by far. He wanted nothing greater than to see Him for whom his soul longed.

Johann Franck was a German lawyer, poet, and hymn writer living in the seventeenth century. In a famous hymn, he expressed the hedonistic pleasure he found in Christ in the following lines: "Jesus, priceless treasure, source of purest pleasure, friend most sure and true: long my heart was burning, fainting much and yearning, thirsting, Lord, for you. Yours I am, O spotless Lamb, so will I let nothing hide you, seek no joy beside you!"[19]

I have noticed that as one reads through the book of Revelation, chapters 4, 5, 7, 11, and 15, on to chapter 16, 18, and 19, all have lengthy expressions of praise in them. There can be no doubt that the life to come is filled with events in which the redeemed stand before the throne.

Think of it this way: worship is one of the great privileges that has been given to us. Worship is a celebration of God. When we worship, we celebrate Him and His revealed attributes. We

---

[18] *Desiring God: Meditations of a Christian Hedonist,* John Piper. Colorado Springs, CO: Multnomah Books, 2020

[19] *Jesus, Priceless Treasure,* Johann Frank. 1653

extol who He is and celebrate what He has done. It is a party, a hedonistic feast of holy joy. But worship is also commanded. Psalm 37:4 commands us, "Delight yourself in the Lord." This is a serious command. C. S. Lewis said, "Joy is the serious business of heaven."[20] It is serious because if we choose not to be happy in God, we will reap unhappiness for life. Why?

Happiness leads to praise

First of all, human beings crave happiness. We can't live without it. The French philosopher Blaise Pascal stated, "All men seek happiness. This is without exception. Whatever different means they employ, they all tend to this end. The cause of some going to war, and of others avoiding it, is the same desire in both, attended with different views. The will never takes the least step but to this object. This is the motive of every action of every man, even of those who hang themselves."[21]

Pascal says people commit suicide because they cannot live without being happy. We demand happiness and even fight for it. God created us with the need to be happy. C. S. Lewis said, "But the most obvious fact about praise—whether of God or anything—strangely escaped me. I thought of it in terms of a compliment, approval, or the giving of honour. I had never noticed that all enjoyment spontaneously overflows into praise . . . The world rings with praise—lovers praising their mistresses, readers their favorite poet, walkers praising the countryside, players praising their favorite game . . . I think we delight to praise what we enjoy because the praise not merely expresses but completes the enjoyment; it is its appointed consummation."[22]

You cannot be happy in something without praising it. We cannot be happy in God without praising Him.

---

[20] *Letters to Malcolm: Chiefly on Prayer,* C.S. Lewis. HarperOne, 2017
[21] *Pascal's Pensées,* Blaise Pascal, 1623-1662. New York: E.P. Dutton, 1958
[22] *Reflections on the Psalms,* C.S. Lewis. HarperOne, 2017

John Piper gives an illustration that I have borrowed. Imagine that I came home one night and brought my wife Kathy a bouquet of flowers. She responds by saying, "Why, it's not my birthday, our anniversary, or a special day. To what do I attribute these flowers?" Imagine I said it was my duty to do this on occasion. Merely performing a duty only brings attention to ourselves. And, like all women, my wife would spy out my selfishness.

But now, imagine the same scenario from a different perspective. What if I said, "I brought you these flowers because as I thought of you I was overwhelmed with your beauty, the joy you have brought me, and the love I have for you. I just felt that the joy I find in you was not complete unless I found a way of expressing that. It is true that these flowers can't truly express what I feel, but they express a part of what I am bursting to say."

This is an apt description of worship. The loveliness of God can't be experienced without some way of expressing the experience of joy that we find in God.

God is like no other

Show me someone who cannot enter into worship out of a motivation for joy and I will show you someone who has never delighted themselves in the Lord. We were created for relationship with God. That relationship expresses itself in worship. Worship is finding pleasure in God. And this pleasure eventually leads to a consummation, where we see God face to face in glory.

Revelation 22:4 says, "They will see his face." I have often struggled with what this could possibly mean. If I were to ask you, "What does God look like?" what would you say? Does God have a body as we do? Is there any matter or physicality to God? Or is He pure energy? What are we talking about when we talk about God?

According to the Bible, none of those things are right. In John 4:24, Jesus said, "God is spirit." What can that mean? As we read through the Old Testament, we see the matter spelled out. For instance, in the Ten Commandments the second command forbids the making of carved images or any likeness in Heaven or on earth made to represent God. Then in Deuteronomy 4:12 we are told, "Then the LORD spoke to you out of the midst of the fire. You heard the sound of words, but saw no form, there was only a voice." Those words are later repeated in the form of a command in verses 15–17: "Therefore watch yourselves very carefully. Since you saw no form on the day that the LORD spoke to you at Horeb out of the midst of the fire, beware lest you act corruptly by making a carved image for yourselves, in the form of any figure, the likeness of male or female, the likeness of any animal that is on the earth, the likeness of any winged bird that flies in the air."

From these passages we learn that we should not think of God as having a physical form of any kind. God is essentially different from all that He has created. To make an image—any image—is to fundamentally misrepresent God. Indeed, when the second command is given, God adds the words, "For I the LORD your God am a jealous God." God is jealous for His honour and jealous that He is not misrepresented. He is angered when we think of Him other than He is.

And so, unlike us, God has no physical body. He is not made of matter like the rest of His creation. We should not think of Him as energy, vapour, air, or space. And we certainly should not think of Him as a man of some sort. Instead, as Jesus taught us, "God is spirit."

This means that He is unlike all other things. Much of what we learn is through comparisons. A child gets a book on animals and soon learns that birds and mammals and reptiles fit into various categories. A stork looks different from a hummingbird, but they share certain characteristics. It is in comparison with similar things that we build categories and begin to understand our world.

But there are no categories in which God can be compared. He is unlike every other thing. That is why Isaiah 46:5 says, "To whom will you liken me and make me equal, and compare me, that we may be alike?"

There is nothing like God.

To say that God is spirit is to say that He is not made of matter, has no parts or dimensions, and we are unable to appreciate Him with any of our bodily senses. There is, in fact, nothing for our eyes to see.

Some of us will point to passages such as Isaiah 6 where the prophet said, "I saw the LORD." But as John tells us in John 12:41, "Isaiah said these things because he saw Christ's glory." The miracle of the incarnation is that God the Son, who, like all members of the Trinity, is also spirit, clothed Himself in human flesh and dwelt among us. He took upon himself the form of a man.

That in itself requires a great deal of care to unpack. It staggers the mind that God should take on human flesh. However, this truth must not obscure the truth that the Father has no form, and there is nothing for our eyes to see.

The mystery of seeing Him face to face

What then can it possibly mean that we will see His face in Heaven, as John tells us in Revelation 22:4? I have pondered this mystery for a long time. I know that earlier, in Revelation 4, John declares that he saw a door open in Heaven. He then speaks of a throne. But when he refers to He who is seated on that throne, John mentions brightness and colours as well as the sea of glass that surrounds the throne, but he avoids any description of the Almighty himself. Then he mentions lightning and thunder and the four living creatures crying "holy."

Here we are led to a fascinating mystery. What will we actually see when the book of Revelation tells us we will see God?

Perhaps Augustine, the great theologian from the fourth century, had it right: "It is thoroughly credible, that we shall in the future world see the material forms of the new heavens and the new earth in such a way that we shall most distinctly recognise God everywhere present and governing all things, material as well as spiritual...God will be so known by us, and shall be so much before us, that we shall see Him by the spirit in ourselves, in one another, in Himself, in the new heavens and the new earth, in every created thing which shall then exist; and also by the body we shall see Him in every body which the keen vision of the eye of the spiritual body shall reach."[23]

Perhaps there will be an ability to see the hand of the Father in all things in a way that we never thought possible. But Revelation does seem to bring us to a place where the central focus is worship. Whether that place is seen in the colours of jasper and carnelian and emeralds and of an amazing sense of light that makes all other light but a facsimile of the real thing, we will be there to see Him.

Around the throne will be the twenty-four elders. There will be four living creatures. There will be the 144,000 and a great multitude that no one can number. We might all remember Genesis 15. There was a day when God and Abraham went for a walk on a clear, cloudless night. God had said to Abraham, "Look into the sky and count the stars." If you have been out of the city where there is no light pollution, you know what that looks like: Orion, the Great Bear, Pleiades, the vast Milky Way, with seemingly endless brilliant lights. God said, "Go ahead, Abraham, and count the stars." Abraham responds, "I can't, for there are too many." And God responds, "So shall your offspring be."

When John stood before the throne, Revelation 7:9–10 describes what he saw (and what we too will see): "And behold,

---

[23] *The City of God (Vol 2)*. St Augustine. Project Gutenberg, 2014

a great multitude that no one could number, from every nation, from all tribes and peoples and languages standing before the throne and before the Lamb, clothed in white robes, with palm branches in their hands, and crying with a loud voice, 'Salvation belongs to our God who sits on the throne, and to the Lamb.'"

I don't know exactly how this matter plays out, but I would like to share what I see in my imagination. When we live on the new earth, we will learn to do all things to the glory of God. Whether it is creating or building or art or politics or science, every activity will be to showcase the excellency of our God.

But then there will be sacred moments. Psalms 120–134 contains a grouping of Psalms called *The Songs of Ascent.* They were sung by pilgrims on their way to Jerusalem during high times of worship, like Passover or the Feast of Weeks or the Day of Atonement. As the pilgrims approached Jerusalem, the city came into sight, and as they went down the Kidron Valley and ascended the other side, these psalms represent not only their singing, but also their great joy as they approached the Holy City. They would sing Psalm 122: "I was glad when they said to me, 'Let us go to the house of the LORD!'" Or they would sing Psalm 125: "Those who trust in the LORD are like Mount Zion which cannot be moved, but abides forever." Or Psalm 124: "If it had not been the LORD who was on our side when people rose up against us, then they would have swallowed us up alive."

And as the pilgrims sang, all were filled with joy. I imagine that in the world to come, perhaps there are special days for worship. We will approach the Holy City and break into songs of joy and anticipation. Then the redeemed will stand before the One who sits on the throne and the Lamb, and we will shout to them with a collective roar from the countless multitude.

More than anything else, this is the undying hope of all the people of God!

CHAPTER THIRTEEN

RULING AND REIGNING WITH CHRIST

I don't know what comes to your mind when you think about politics, but it's hard to deny a growing attitude of cynicism from the general public. For reasons both good and bad, people are losing confidence in the system, and that bodes ill for all of us. It seems clear things need to change. If not, we invite disillusionment, despair or even worse, revolution. Politics and politicians have been receiving a bad rap for some time now. One can tell this is the case by the words people use. "That's politics," they say. This is almost never a compliment. "You are behaving like a politician" means you should be ashamed of yourself, or you are being insincere.

Some would add, "Well, praise God we won't have politicians in Heaven." Are they right? If you side with that sentiment, I fear I have bad news for you. The idea of the governance of Heaven, or the system of government employed in Heaven, often strikes people as strange indeed.

According to Revelation 22:5, speaking of the age to come, John comments on the nature of Heaven: "And the night will be no more. They will need no light of lamp or sun, for the Lord God will be their light, and they will reign forever and ever." Everything in John's description seems to agree with our sensibilities until we hear that we will reign forever and ever. We could translate that to accurately say, "We will exercise governance forever," or the passage could read, "We will be a part of the political structure of Heaven forever and ever."

Is this a solitary text, or is this idea found in other locations in the Bible? It may surprise some to discover that this is a familiar theme often repeated throughout the New Testament. In Revelation 2:26–27, Jesus's message to the church in Thyatira is, "The one who conquers and who keeps my works until the end, to him I will give authority over the nations and he will rule them with a rod of iron, as when earthen pots are broken in pieces, even as I myself have received authority from my Father."

That is a magnificent thought containing a string of phrases about our activities in Heaven. Many of the phrases John employs come out of Psalm 2:6–9, where the Messiah will be given authority over all nations and break them with a rod of iron. I think the promise given to the church in Thyatira is most likely a picture of Christ's millennial rule. We might get a picture here of Jesus ruling the nations He defeats at Armageddon and of the subsequent millennial Kingdom. Jesus promises the church of Thyatira, a church hard-pressed by persecution, His impending victory over all His enemies. When that victory is secured, His own people will share the responsibility of ruling the defeated nations with Him. Again we are to think of the thousand-year reign of Christ prior to the final judgment. During this era, the saints will have a particular role to play. They will actively participate in the political reign of Jesus the Messiah.

Here is a word to the church in Laodicea: "The one who conquers, I will grant him to sit with me on my throne, as I also conquered and sat down with my Father on his throne" (Revelation 3:21). Here the reference is not to the Old Testament, but to a direct teaching given by Jesus to the twelve disciples: "Jesus said to them, 'Truly, I say to you, in the new world, when the Son of Man will sit on his glorious throne, you who have followed me will also sit on twelve thrones, judging the twelve tribes of Israel. And everyone who has left houses or brothers or sisters or father or mother or children or lands, for my name's sake, will receive a hundredfold and will inherit eternal life'" (Matthew 19:28–29).

There are two things for us to notice. First, Jesus promises the twelve a role of prominence in judging the twelve tribes of Israel. However, in Revelation Jesus opens the privilege of reigning with Him over all the nations He has conquered at His Second Coming. Again we think of the millennium. Second, Jesus seems to indicate that anyone who has sacrificed anything for His name and the gospel while here on earth will receive a hundredfold return on that investment in Heaven or in the life to come. There He is clearly referring to the time of the new heavens and the new earth.

Further on, in Revelation 5:9b–10, we see that not only are those who hope on Him saved by the blood of Christ, but that Christ also bestows on His followers a future role in which they govern the earth. Speaking of Jesus, that text says, "You were slain, and by your blood you ransomed people for God from every tribe and language and people and nation, and you have made them a kingdom and priests to our God and they shall reign on the earth." Here, the reference seems to be the new heavens and earth.

There are passages in Scripture outside of Revelation that speak this way as well. For example, Paul speaks of it in 2 Timothy 2:12: "If we endure, we will also reign with him." Romans 8:16-17 says, "The Spirit himself bears witness with our spirit that we are children of God, and if children, then heirs—heirs of God and fellow heirs with Christ." Clearly, the Bible makes plain that everything that belongs to Christ is also given to us, His people. The only exception is the divinity of

Christ. In this matter, He alone rules. However, the saints will be included in His rule.

It is clear from the Bible that we will participate in some way with God's governance. But lest we think of this as a matter restricted to the earth, we have not yet seen the promise for what it is: we will rule with Christ over all the works of His hands. And if we think this is only a promise related to the millennium, Revelation 22:5, in speaking of the new heavens and earth and our final state, says that we shall reign with him forever and ever.

But how are we to understand these promises specifically?

Consider God's original intent in creation. In Genesis 1, after God had created the man and the woman, He gave them their very first command: "Be fruitful and multiply and fill the earth and subdue it, and have dominion [have rulership, governance, authority over] the fish of the sea and over the birds of the heavens and over every living thing that moves on the earth." As image-bearers of God, the man, the woman, and their offspring were to fill the earth and rule it. *Ruling* refers to governance. They were to direct the affairs of the creation according to the design of the Creator.

Initially, we see the expression of this in the naming that Adam does of all the creatures in Genesis 2:19. The act of naming is an act of expressing authority over something or someone that is being named. For instance, in the book of Daniel, Nebuchadnezzar names Daniel and his three friends. He changes their Jewish names for Babylonian ones. In so doing he is expressing authority over them. He has determined their identity. He also determines what they are to become, and the activities that will now mark their lives.

That is what Adam is doing in his first activity. But he is also doing more. Naming involves a level of understanding. When we name something, we are engaging in the beginning of the scientific enterprise. Naming has to do with observation. Adam demonstrates that he has the beginning of an understanding of the functions inherent in the animals. He is ascertaining what God had in mind when He created them, and also how they are to be governed.

Isn't it interesting then that when Satan comes to tempt the man and the woman, he enters the garden as a serpent? He is a creature that God has made. Given Adam's mandate, we would then assume that he is required to demonstrate his understanding of the serpent, as well as his authority over it. Adam would have known that he was master over the serpent. Instead, in a horrible tragedy, he surrenders his authority to him. With that he becomes not the ruler, but the one who struggles to survive. The serpent uses his advantage against the God-appointed ruler of the creation. Alienated from God now, the serpent seeks the complete destruction of the human race.

The Good News expressed in Genesis 3:15 is that God would send a seed of the woman to crush the head of the serpent and rightfully reclaim all that was lost in the Fall. This, of course, is the drama of the story of Jesus. His authority would be to restore that which Adam had lost. For this reason, the command to rule over the works of God's hands is not lost but has been redeemed. According to Romans 5, Jesus is the second Adam, the new federal head of those who reclaimed what Adam had lost.

Therefore, whatever the Bible means by ruling and reigning with Christ in eternity must be related to the original plan given to Adam: rule over the works of God's hands.

The command to rule is related to the covenant God made with Abraham. In Genesis 12 God makes a covenant with one man, to whom he promises three things. First, He promises to bless him. That would mean that God covenants to allow all the resources He has as God to be used for Abraham's benefit. That in itself is an overwhelming promise. Second, God promises to make of Abraham a great nation, more than can be numbered. Finally, God promises to give Abraham and his offspring a land flowing with the blessings of his creation—it will flow with milk and honey.

Of course, the Old Testament is clear that this is the land of Israel. The descendants of Abraham are called upon to take the land God has promised them. They are to exercise dominion over it by driving pagan worshippers from it and rule that land as representatives of God. That is the drama of the book of Joshua and of the kingdom of David. It is the struggle to rule and reign over that which God has promised.

What the Old Testament can teach us about our life in Heaven

Can we take the drama of the Old Testament and apply that to our activities in eternity?

There are those of us who have wondered whether ruling with Christ relates to actual real estate. To some, that sounds crassly commercial. We imagine a landlord, seizing land and holding it. Are we to think of a physical land over which the saints rule?

The answer to that question can be found in an often-neglected passage from the Old Testament: Jeremiah, chapter 32. Jeremiah has been prophesying that Jerusalem would be destroyed by the Babylonians because of their sins. This takes place during the tenth year of Zedekiah's reign, which would have been less than one year until the Babylonians would destroy Jerusalem and seize all the land of Israel as their own. At the time of Jeremiah's writing, the Babylonian armies are surrounding the city, besieging it. The future looks hopeless. For Israel, surely death, destruction, and the dissolution of the nation lies before them.

"Jeremiah said, 'The word of the LORD came to me: Behold, Hanamel the son of Shallum your uncle will come to you and say, "Buy my field that is at Anathoth, for the right of redemption by purchase is yours"''" (Jeremiah 32:6-7). Anathoth was about five kilometres north of Jerusalem. No doubt, at the very moment Jeremiah was buying this property, the boots of Babylonian soldiers were standing on the very ground he was buying. From the perspective of what was happening, this purchase was ludicrous. In less than a year—and Jeremiah knew this—Judah would be taken into exile and the land he was purchasing would be under the dominion of Babylon. Why buy that which is in effect worthless?

Next, God reiterates to Jeremiah that His anger is provoked against Jerusalem for their sins. And yet, at a time in the future Israel will return to their land. In that future time, God declares, "Fields shall be bought for money, and deeds shall be signed and sealed and witnessed, in the land of Benjamin, in the places about Jerusalem and in the cities of Judah" (Jeremiah 32:44). God will restore their fortunes. Nothing has been lost. God will redeem all that has been stolen because of sin. God promises He will redeem it all.

At first reading, one can be excused for thinking this promise relates entirely to the return of the exiles and the resettlement of the land under Ezra and Nehemiah, until one reads the next chapter of Jeremiah. There God promises that a branch, the Messiah, will rule in Jerusalem and execute justice. In this time, Jerusalem will dwell securely. The image of Jeremiah buying a field points to the time when the Messiah, not the Babylonians nor the Persians, would rule the land. That is when men and women will take possession of houses and lands. And that is what Jeremiah was doing in his purchase. He was buying property to be owned during the reign of the Messiah.

Consider Jesus's parable of the ten minas in Luke 19. There He makes promises to One who is faithful. In the days when the king receives his kingdom, the faithful servant will be put in charge over ten cities. Still another will be put over five cities. As strange as this language sounds to us, we must think about the new heavens and the new earth as real, physical places. The Kingdom to come will also have citizens who have physical bodies. Therefore, they will be required to live somewhere. For this reason, we must think of literal houses and lands and properties and the administration of such things. Jeremiah, in a symbolic act, secured his own property in the days to come.

I often ask a question to people I teach about Heaven: "If Adam and Eve had never sinned, would we need laws?" Invariably, everyone answers by saying that we would not. But then I challenge that way of thinking. In an unfallen world, would we still need to have laws that tell us on which side of the road to drive? Unfortunately, most think that the only function of law is to restrain evil. In the present order of things, that is true. Paul tells us that God ordains that rulers in the present day would be a terror to wrongdoers. Good societies are to function in this way.

Clearly those laws will forever be unnecessary in the world to come. But in the world that will soon be revealed, laws will be enacted to maximize the good to all and enhance the glory of God.

Ruling with Christ

What does ruling and reigning with Christ look like? If you go back to a verse that we often quote at Christmas, we will see a wonderful secret. According to Isaiah 9:7, "Of the increase of his government and of peace there will be no end." As time goes on, the government of Christ will not be static, but will increase. Does that sound strange? How can His government increase? Does this indicate that His government is not complete in the new age?

In Daniel 7:21-22, we are told of the time when the saints possessed the Kingdom. Then later, in verse 27 of the same chapter, an explanation is given of that picture: "And the kingdom and the dominion and the greatness of the kingdoms under the whole heaven shall be given to the people of the saints of the most high; their kingdom shall be an everlasting kingdom and all dominions shall serve and obey them." A picture is now forming. Jesus progressively expands His government through His people, in which all the dominions are governed and serve and obey Christ through the governance of His people.

In Revelation 21:22–26, John gives us a vision of the Holy City. The New Jerusalem comes down out of Heaven to earth:

> And I saw no temple in the city, for its temple is the Lord God the Almighty and the Lamb. And the city has no need of sun or moon to shine on it, for the glory of God gives it light, and its lamp is the Lamb. By its light will the nations walk, and kings of the earth will bring their glory into it, and its gates will never be shut by day—and there will be no night there. They will bring into it the glory and honour of the nations.

Imagine an earth filled with various cultures and governors or kings. All of the cultures that make up the new heavens and earth need to be governed. Furthermore, the rulers of the earth come into the Holy City, bringing the best of their cultural achievements, and lay them at the feet of Jesus in honour and praise to their great King. They wish to acknowledge that all they accomplished was to celebrate Him. As their cultures develop over time, they keep striving for more ways to honour and glorify the one who sits on the throne and the Lamb.

Imagine a new earth that has culture, accomplishments, inventions, and splendour that is unique to groups of people. Imagine the profound creativity of that. Imagine not a world of competition, but one that seeks to glorify God.

What else is there?

But is this it? Are we only to govern one another? No, it is not. According to Randy Alcorn, commenting on the expansion of the government of the Messiah found in Isaiah 9:7, "We are called upon as the saints to expand into previously ungoverned territories."[24] Another task is to create new territories. This, he suggests, could be new planets or new realms under Christ's rulership.

Is this simply fantasy, or even a part of what God has prepared? Interestingly, Alcorn is not the only one to think this way. Erwin Lutzer, long-time pastor of the famous Moody Bible Church in Chicago, said, "The discovery of the immensity of the universe does not diminish but actually magnifies man's role in the cosmos. For if Christ is to rule over all things, and we are to reign with Him, then we will be ruling over all the galaxies affirming Christ's Lordship over the whole universe."[25] Dr. Joseph Dillow, former professor at Dallas Theological Seminary, reflected on Psalm 8:6, which says that God has given man dominion over the works of his hands. He believes that this psalm includes all the works of God's fingers. This must include the sun, moon, and stars. He says, "The future kingdom embraces the entire created order that this was to be placed in subjection to man."[26]

Clearly, when we think of Heaven, we can no longer imagine an endless vacation in which we plan on living at the edge of a golf course, sipping fruit drinks and eating caviar. We should think of a physical life in a physical world, with a God of glory we worship who gives His followers visionary tasks that fill our hearts with joy.

---

[24] *Heaven,* Randy Alcorn. Carol Stream, IL: Tyndale House Publishers, 2004
[25] *Heaven and the Afterlife,* Erwin W. Lutzer. Moody Publishers, 2016
[26] *Final Destiny,* Joseph Dillow. Grace Theology Press, 2018

I end this chapter on ruling with Christ with the words of Jesus. Luke 16:10 records Jesus as saying, "One who is faithful in a very little is also faithful in much, and one who is dishonest in a very little is also dishonest in much."

Our life on earth in this present time is connected to the life to come. This is only a training ground for ruling. This present life offers but the first lessons in our task to trust Christ and redound all glory to Him. And as we learn this lesson well, we are being trained for our role in eternity.

Playing harps on a bland, lifeless cloud forever? Most certainly not. Ruling and reigning with Christ for all of eternity? Yes! Begin to develop an appetite now, so that you can hardly wait for it to begin.

CHAPTER FOURTEEN

GOING ON FOR ETERNITY

When my future wife Kathy and I were getting close to our wedding day, we had a conversation about what the theme of our wedding should be. We thought it should also be the theme for our life together as husband and wife. We could think of no better verse than Micah 4:5: "For all the peoples walk each in the name of its god, but we will walk in the name of the LORD our God forever and ever." We both felt strongly that this verse was the theme of our lives. We would build our life together and whatever family that God would give us on the foundation of walking in the name of Yahweh our God. But as many years have now come and gone, I have been thinking more and more about the words "forever and ever." That is not to say that I expect to be married to Kathy in eternity. Jesus was quite clear on this matter. In Matthew 22:30, He said, "For in the resurrection they neither marry nor are given in marriage." Marriage is a temporary matter, designed only for the present life.

But I am taken up in the thought that Kathy and I will walk in the name of the Lord forever. Surely our relationship in the new heavens and earth will be changed, but I am reminded that what we committed to Him will not cease. We will walk in the name of the Lord forever. And although it will not be a marriage relationship, it will indeed be a relationship. And it will continue to have a faithfulness to Christ at its core.

I am reminded of a conversation I had with my father as he lay on his deathbed. We were talking about Heaven, but our conversation ranged over a number of topics. At one time he told me that he would love to take one more hike in the mountains. Dad loved the mountains of western British Columbia. I said to him, "Dad, in the world to come, I want to hike the mountains with you." He smiled. Our relationship would continue.

I mention my wedding vows and the deathbed of my father because I, along with all believers, know the promises God has made are altogether enduring. Forever and ever. Nothing of importance is lost to the believer in death. I wish to repeat the line, so my reader does not pass by it too quickly: nothing of importance is lost to the believer in death.

Some believers are not sure of that. The sense of loss that death brings seems overwhelming. As they think of death, their minds are taken up by what will be no more. But are they right to think this way? Let's divide our thinking on this matter into two sections.

1. Death cannot take away our essential humanity

Let's be sure of what is definitely not lost. Here I address those matters that all believers will immediately recognize.

First, let's remember the things that death cannot take from a believer. Job discusses it in Job 19:26: "And after my skin has been thus destroyed, yet in my flesh I will see God." In this study we have already examined the glorious biblical truth that Christ will raise our physical bodies. Our resurrection body will be both our self-same body and also made to be like Christ's resurrection body. Indeed, we will have our body forever. It will, however, be a body that will never perish. Paul called it an "imperishable body." Furthermore, essential to our human experience is the image of God in us. This includes our abilities to think and reason. We will be fully human as we feel emotion and experience the full range of what this means. We will enjoy friendship and form lasting memories.

I am often asked questions about Heaven. Will we remember our life on earth? I often respond by saying that Heaven is not like the belief in reincarnation. There is a full continuity between the life on earth and the one to come. For this reason, it should be a matter of common sense. Of course we will remember our past life. Memories are a part of our humanity and give the importance of continuity. How, for instance, are we to worship the Christ who died for us if we could not remember what He died for?

Some people are troubled by that thought. They wonder about the painful, even humiliating memories they struggle with today. What if we maintain the memories of our sins and failures? Would this not trouble or shame us in Heaven? I think it's quite the opposite. Without our minds being clouded by sin, we will remember with greater insight as well as with redeemed thinking. Whenever we think of past sins while on earth, we will marvel at the grace of Christ. Whenever we remember our past wounds and hurts, we will see them through the eyes of Romans 8:28 and see with penetrating insight how these things served to maximize our joy in the life we now enjoy. Our death will not remove our essential humanity from us, nor will it remove our unique experience of being ourselves.

2. Death cannot take away our enjoyment of life

When I ask believers what they think won't be there after they die, one of the common answers is, "Time will be no more." I always respond by asking, "Why do you think that?" Some remember the King James Version of Revelation 10:6, where it says there will be no more time. But that is not the best translation of the original Greek. What is really expressed in that passage is that there will be no more delay in the fulfilling of the purposes of God.

Others remember the old hymn, "When the Roll Is Called up Yonder." It begins with the words, *When the trumpet of the Lord shall sound and time shall be no more.*[27] Please remember that those are words in a hymnal and not in your Bible. Sadly, not everything the Church has sung over the years accurately reflects the teachings of the scripture.

Others have said, "Yes, but isn't God beyond time?" Yes, He is. However, God created time. Time is His invention. He stands outside of time, even as He stands apart from all of His creation. Unlike paganism, the living God is not identified as a part of the creation, though God is actively engaged in every aspect of it. So it is with time. God created it and wishes it to remain.

We as human beings are not God. We will never be God. God is infinite, we are not. We are finite. Hence, we will always live within time.

There are other things about God that we will not share. God is omniscient, but we will never know all things. We will learn and grow and progress throughout eternity. When we hear people sometimes remarking that in Heaven we will know all things, I believe they are wrong. Omniscience is an essential attribute of God. It is an attribute that He does not share with His creation. We will learn and grow and progress. This takes time. To those who ask how it will be possible to continue to learn new things for eternity, we think this to be short-sighted. How could we ever exhaust the riches of the knowledge of God? We won't. Only God is infinite. We are finite beings. For these reasons, I believe that the experience of time as a succession of moments will still be our experience in eternity.

---

[27] *When the Roll Is Called Up Yonder,* James M. Black. 1893.

Consider the evidence of this in scripture. If you go back to the covenant God made with Noah, Genesis 8:22 says, "While the earth remains, seedtime and harvest, cold and heat, summer and winter, day and night shall never cease." Of course, this is a promise that God gave Noah, assuring him that the earth will never again be destroyed by a flood. We might say that the progression of seasons on this earth may not be repeated in the world to come. But I would argue that God has promised that seasons do carry on in the next world.

Time in the earth/time to come

Let's see if we find any of those markers of the progress of time in the earth to come. We'll start with the promise God makes in the last chapter of Isaiah: "For as the new heavens and the new earth that I make shall remain before me, says the LORD, so shall your offspring and your name remain. From new moon to new moon, and from Sabbath to Sabbath, all flesh shall come to worship before me, declares the LORD" (Isaiah 66:22–23).

That statement seems to indicate a rhythm of life. Isaiah mentions new moons, weekly Sabbaths, and set times of worship. Those words seem familiar, don't they? They sound like the experience of time we enjoy now.

Consider the evidence from the end of Revelation: "Then the angel showed me the river of the water of life, bright as crystal, flowing from the throne of God and of the Lamb through the middle of the street of the city; also, on either side of the river, the tree of life with its twelve kinds of fruit, yielding its fruit each month" (Revelation 22:1–2).

Notice some of the features of that description of the life to come. First, note the spatial dimensions. Water is flowing from the throne to the middle of the street. That describes both the distance and time required to flow for that distance. Also notice the variety of things that are described, even to the variety of available food. Then note the reference to months—twelve are mentioned. This means that the marking of time is very much the way we do it today. We see a description of seasons and years. The tree in the centre of the city has seasons in which a different fruit is in season that year. It is a most remarkable tree.

From what we have read, this begins to sound very much like the promise God gave to Noah. He was promised that the seasons and years will not cease. If we want further examples of time in Heaven, we might consider Revelation 8:1, where we are told there is silence in Heaven. Then we are told the length of time of the silence: about one half hour. Or we might consider Revelation 7:15, where we are told of the saints who come out of the great tribulation. These saints serve God day and night.

A careful reader might object, "Aren't we being over-literal? After all, Revelation 21:25 says there will never be night in the New Jerusalem." However—and this is fascinating—the city itself has no need for sun to shine on it. The reason the sun is absent has nothing to do with the experience of time. The reason is that the glory of God in the city is so overwhelming that the sun would seem like a dim light indeed. However, the experience inside the Holy City is not representative of what is experienced in the rest of the new creation. There we are told that day and night carry on.

Without indulging in endless speculation of whether we will experience the rhythms of sleep and wake in the world to come, we can be sure of this: the Bible does speak of the rhythm of seasons, and even of the weekly celebration of stopping everything in order that we might worship.

When we think about the life that God has reserved for the objects of His mercy, we must picture a world in which we lose nothing of what brought us joy here. What do you think you will miss of this sin-cursed earth that we presently live on? A cup of coffee in the morning? The sensation of the sun on your face? A hug and a smile from an old dear friend? Curling up by the fire with a book in hand? Hiking through the mountains and breathing in the fresh clean cold air? Love and friendship? An evening study of scripture and the Word of God? Coming to the house of worship and bowing in reverence or singing for joy to the King of Kings and Lord of Lords? None of these things are lost!

But does that mean we lose nothing? No, as a matter of fact, there are some glorious losses ahead of us.

Glorious losses

I am thinking about a well-known quotation by C. S. Lewis, taken from his book *The Weight of Glory*. "It would seem," said Lewis, "that Our Lord finds our desires not too strong, but too weak. We are half-hearted creatures, fooling about with drink and sex and ambition when infinite joy is offered us, like an ignorant child who wants to go on making mud pies in a slum because he cannot imagine what is meant by the offer of a holiday at the sea. We are far too easily pleased."[28]

Indeed, I think we are. Weeping that we will lose this world is like the child who weeps incessantly that he is taken from a muddy backyard sandbox to go to the wonder of a warm stretch of white ocean sand and stunning vistas. Why is it then that believers fear death so much? Why have I stood at the bedside of dying believers who have told me they really didn't want to die at all? And why is it that believers sometimes feel sorrow at how horrible it was that a loved one in Christ is no more? Of course we weep over the gravity of this temporary loss, but what is it that makes some even shake their fists at God, wondering why it is that He would have allowed this person to die?

I believe I know the answer to this phenomenon: we know so little of Heaven. Even what we think we know may be wrong.

---

[28] *The Weight of Glory*, C.S. Lewis. HarperOne, 2015

We have allowed popular images of Heaven to overshadow the revelation from God's inerrant word. So many believe that those who have died in Christ have had something of significance taken from them. Instead, we ought to rejoice over the passing of a loved one, even as we weep over the painful loss we feel by their departure. But we should revel, knowing that nothing of significance has been lost. Rather, something of great significance has been gained.

In order to recover perspective, let's recite what is lost to us at death

Years ago, my wife wrote a letter to a work colleague. We were moving, and Kathy knew she would never see her colleague and friend again. The woman was not a believer, but Kathy had spoken to her in the past of Christ and His amazing grace. Kathy's last letter to this woman referred to Christ's promise for His elect in Heaven. Revelation 21:4 promises, "He will wipe away every tear from their eyes, and death shall be no more, neither shall there be mourning, nor crying, nor pain anymore, for the former things have passed away." In her letter, Kathy told her friend that if she wasn't there in Heaven, Kathy would be heartbroken. Christ would have to wipe the tears of sorrow from her eyes, for she would need solace from such pain in the arms of her Redeemer.

I have spoken with parents who have told me they cannot imagine any greater pain than to arrive in glory and find a child missing. And for some of us, the idea of going to Heaven without the assurance that those we have loved have made peace with God is almost more than we can bear. What comfort can be given to those of you who weep over these matters?

What I now write will require time to settle in. I warn you that you may be angry with the following lines. But I plead with you, carefully and prayerfully read the lines to come.

The thing about Heaven that excites me more than anything else is that, finally and ultimately, I will love what God loves. Furthermore, I will also be overwhelmed that all of God's ways and deeds are vindicated in the end. Those who savour the loveliness of Christ will not look at those who have been eternally damned and wonder how God could have allowed such a thing to happen. Rather, we will look carefully into the matters of grace and of justice, and we will marvel that all of God's ways are right and good. And we will love His ways. This is the answer to the loss of the unrepentant.

Consider carefully the words of scripture, recorded in 2 Thessalonians 1:9–10: "They will suffer the punishment of eternal destruction, away from the presence of the Lord and from the glory of his might, when he comes on that day to be glorified in his saints, and to be marveled at among all who have believed." It would seem that God's perfect justice, even in the damnation of the wicked, is cause for the saints to overflow with praise, wonder, amazement, and overwhelming love for a God who does all things for His glory and the greatness of His name. The saints will worship. They will not rub their hands in glee over the fate of the lost, but they will overflow with wonder as the altogether righteous God expresses splendour in the rightful judgment of the damned.

This is not to say that we are callous in Heaven. I am reminded of Jesus riding into Jerusalem on Palm Sunday, knowing that it would end in the destruction of that city. They had rejected the day of His visitation. And so, as Jesus triumphally rides into Jerusalem to bring all of history to the point of climax, He also weeps. But weeping and compassion, in the mind of Jesus, never ends up in lazy sentimentalism. Jesus's greatest desire was for God to be glorified above all other things.

When we see Jesus in Heaven, we will love, above all other things, the outpouring of God's glory. We will marvel that all His attributes, even in the great damnation that will come upon many, will showcase the glory, greatness, power, and loveliness of all that He does. And we will long for no greater thing in all eternity than that the holiness of God should shine in splendour.

All relationships in Heaven will centre on this glory. And because of our longing to enter ever more deeply into the splendour of the character and the deeds of Heaven, we will be overwhelmed and joyful. Nothing will steal that joy. In Revelation 18 and 19, the saints before the throne sing with joy because, according to Revelation 19:2, "his judgments are true and just," even when He condemns the unredeemed.

That might answer some of our questions, even as it is difficult for us to hear of it. But knowing that there lies before all of us the great realities of Heaven and Hell should make us pray more fervently here. We should entreat God for the salvation of the lost and boldly witness to the saving message of Jesus. But above all, let's not let lesser views of the glory of God twist the truths that there lies before every human being Heaven or Hell. Let's let the biblical witness speak, and let us be content that in Heaven we will have no greater joy than to know He who is altogether glorious and lovely.

What else might we miss in Heaven? Will we miss marriage? We will not. The life God has prepared for us will include the richness of intimate relationships with others. Yes, the sexual act is forever left behind. But there is a pure pleasure that awaits that will remind us that marriage was but a shadow and a foretaste of something grander and more fulfilling. We also know that we will not miss the lesser motives we once had in this life that drove us on to dubious accomplishments. We will not miss sin, pain, debt, envy, loneliness, and the constant rebellion against the plans of God. And I will certainly not miss death or pain or mourning or weeping.

We will remember all things clearly and miss nothing of the life on earth. We will remember that we have come from the land of shadows into the world of light and colour and vibrancy and righteousness.

In 1 Corinthians 15:55, the apostle Paul asks a question we are now in a position to understand and give an informed answer: "O death, where is your victory? O death, where is your sting?" In the face of such glorious promises, clearly death has lost its power.

If you are facing your own death, dear saint, do not weep. Rejoice in the promises He has given. For you will soon be translated into glory and the life you have always wanted will be yours. And if you are grieving the loss of a loved one—a parent, a child, a brother or sister, a friend, or a colleague—who died in the arms of our loving Saviour, you may weep. However, remember you are weeping for yourself, and not for your loved one. For their lot is better than when you enjoyed fellowship with them. It is better by far.

How important it is to live in the light of hope! Christians have a holy mandate to reject the despair of this world. In place of loss, we grasp firmly to the promises of God and lift up our own heads. Our redemption is drawing near. Each passing year is greeted with anticipation of what lies ahead.

CHAPTER FIFTEEN

CONCLUSION

The first Christian sermon was preached by Peter on the day the Holy Spirit fell and the Church of Jesus Christ was born. As Peter reaches the end of the sermon, his hearers are cut to the heart. Peter then exhorts them to repent from their sins and be baptized in the name of Jesus. And then, to urge them on and help them to understand the gravity of the moment, he says, "Save yourselves from this crooked generation."

Peter's words should startle us. In our times and culture, we expect altar calls to consist of promises that, should we come to Christ, we will inherit a rich, full, and meaningful life. Our sense of alienation from God will end. The purposeless of our lives will evaporate and give way to a life of meaning. This has become the common fashion in which invitations to faith are given. But Peter offers a warning: the present era will eventually give way to a horror. The world and its passions are passing away. The altogether righteous God holds all men accountable. Jesus comes to offer grace to sinners who stand before a yawning abyss: "Save yourselves from this crooked generation. Don't follow the great majority of humanity. Don't tumble into damnation. Awaken and turn from your present pathway."

Talk about Heaven and Hell has been forgotten in the present hour. For this reason, current evangelicalism sounds so very different from the kind of faith we find in the pages of our New Testament. Hebrews 10:30-31 says, "For we know him who said, 'Vengeance is mine; I will repay.' And again, 'The Lord will judge his people.' It is a fearful thing to fall into the hands of the living God."

In His preaching, Jesus depicted a roadway leading to either Heaven or Hell. The broad road leads to destruction. The narrow path leads to life. Hebrews bids us to set aside every weight and the sin which clings so closely. We are to endure and run the race that leads to everlasting life. We are to despise the shame this world inflicts on us, and we are to look to Jesus and to the salvation He offers.

God has made it plain that every life ends in Heaven or Hell. If we live life on our terms, the end is Hell. If we forsake our terms and plead with Jesus for mercy, exchanging our lifestyle for His, we must then fall to our knees and look to Him for grace: "Save us from our sins, for we are sinful beyond cure. Have mercy upon us, for we are lost. But if you look upon our unworthy and damned estate with grace, we will find life."

Romans 5:9 declares, "Since, therefore, we have now been justified by his blood, much more shall we be saved by him from the wrath of God." That's it! We would never be faithful to the Bible account if we did not declare that we were saved from wrath, and saved unto glory.

All of life goes into one of two directions. It leads either to eternal horror or to everlasting splendour. God has put before each of us the way of death and the way of life. Therefore, choose life!

www.ingramcontent.com/pod-product-compliance
Lightning Source LLC
Chambersburg PA
CBHW052142070526
44585CB00017B/1944